ANCIENT ATHENS
ON FIVE DRACHMAS A DAY

*Greek women stand among the columns of a temple porch (*pronaos*).*

PHILIP MATYSZAK

ANCIENT ATHENS
ON FIVE DRACHMAS A DAY

with 72 illustrations, 14 in color

CONTENTS

I · GETTING THERE

Thermopylae § Delphi
Attica § Marathon

THERMOPYLAE

THE GREEK AIR IS FAMOUSLY PURE and clear, so a fortunate traveller will see the beginning of the road to Athens from far across the blue waters of the gulf of Malia, where cloud-topped Mount Oeta looms to the southwest, and ahead lie the cliffs of Thermopylae which guard the gates to southern Greece.

It is spring, so where Mount Kallidromon rises 4,000 feet behind the shoreside cliffs, the oak forests of its lower slopes are clad in fresh, welcoming green. This journey to Athens begins at the point where, a generation ago, another visitor to Greece received a warm welcome at these very appro-priately named 'Hot Gates'. That visitor was Xerxes, the Persian king of kings, accompanied by his myriad soldiers, and here his invasion of Greece suffered its first setback. The Spartan defence of Thermopylae was one of the most famous battles of the Persian wars, and these wars have created the Athens of 431 BC, a city where anything is possible. So it is appropriate that the journey should start at this shore, where Leonidas and his 300 Spartan heroes lie buried.

The first port of call is a tricky landfall on the narrow beach at Anthela. Anthela is a small village tucked into a gorge in the cliffs at the 'west gate', the westernmost of the three narrow passes between

Travelling couple. Their feet are bare – some Athenians spend their lives barefoot.

Horseman. Spears are optional, but crossing bad lands in a large group is the safe choice.

the cliffs and the sea that make up Thermopylae. The first task will be to find lodgings, for even now, over 40 years after the battle, the area attracts a large number of tourists. On occasion these include serious, long-haired gentlemen who have come to visit the grave of their grandfathers. Leonidas, king of Sparta, knew that he was leading his 300 on a suicide mission, and hand-picked his men, choosing only those with living sons to carry on their families. For a few precious days, the Spartans held back the countless thousands of the army of Xerxes while the rest of Greece frantically made ready their defences. The descendants of the 300 could, if they chose, tell the thrilling story of that fight to the death against overwhelming odds. But they probably won't. Spartans are famously laconic. In fact the word was invented for them, meaning 'of Lakonia', the area of Greece where Sparta is situated.

Talk to any ordinary Spartan, and he says so little that he seems to be stupid. Then eventually, like a skilled bowman, he fires off some brief remark that makes you feel positively childish.

PLATO • *PROTAGORAS* • 342

A proper exploration of Thermopylae should begin to the west of Anthela, where the river Sperchios flows into the sea near the Trachinian cliffs. Behind is Mount Oeta, where legend says Herakles (whom the Romans call Hercules) died after completing his famous tasks. His funeral pyre may well have offered a good view of Thermopylae and the final stand of Leonidas, the man believed to be Herakles' direct descendant. The little plain between the river Sperchios and the smaller river Asopus is where the Persians pitched their camp, and from there it is a short walk to the low hill where Xerxes sat watching the battle, occasionally leaping up in shock and anger as the Spartans repeatedly threw back his army.

The fighting itself was further east, past Anthela, where a low spur of Mount

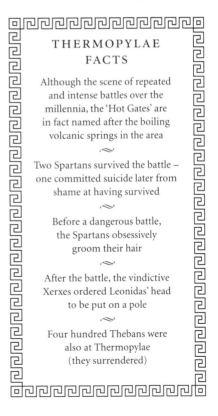

THERMOPYLAE FACTS

Although the scene of repeated and intense battles over the millennia, the 'Hot Gates' are in fact named after the boiling volcanic springs in the area

~

Two Spartans survived the battle – one committed suicide later from shame at having survived

~

Before a dangerous battle, the Spartans obsessively groom their hair

~

After the battle, the vindictive Xerxes ordered Leonidas' head to be put on a pole

~

Four hundred Thebans were also at Thermopylae (they surrendered)

Kallidromon widens the pass to a relatively wide 30 yards or so. Here, at the 'middle gate', there is a ruined wall where the Greeks originally made their stand. Later, when all was lost, they fell back to the east and fought to the death on a low hill, where a stone lion now stands in their memory.

Further along, three marble pillars stand near the 'east gate'. The first contains a verse to the memory of Megistias the seer, who foresaw disaster yet chose to stay with the 300. It was written by Megistias' friend Simonides, the great elegiac poet who lived in Athens until his death 20 years after the battle.

You see here the great Megistias' tomb
Who slew the Medes, fresh from Sperchios'
fords.
The wise seer clearly foresaw his death,
Yet would not forsake the Spartan cause.
SIMONIDES

The second pillar commemorates all the Greeks who fought in the battle: 'Four thousand, who held back millions'. The last is for Leonidas' men alone, and carries the simple message. 'Go, traveller, tell the Spartans that we died here, obeying our orders.'

After viewing these memorials, return if there is time to a point by the twisting path across Mount Kallidromon. This path is called Anopaea, a name it shares both with the hill over which it runs and with the river that accompanies the path back to the sea. Here you will retrace the steps of the 5,000 Persian Immortals

who outflanked, and so consequently doomed, Leonidas' force. Somewhat oddly, amidst the grandeur of this tragic drama, the tour of Thermopylae ends at a smooth outcrop of rocks known to locals as 'the black buttocks'.

Back in Anthela it is time to procure a donkey and pack a cloak (Greeks are unfussy, minimalist dressers – this cloak, called a *himaton*, is all that some of your fellow travellers will be wearing). You also need sturdy boots, a wide hat and food to sustain you on your journey to Delphi. It is time to meet the Greek road, and to discover why serious travellers in Greece go by sea whenever possible.

DELPHI

THE ROAD (IF THIS WINDING mountain track deserves such a name) takes the traveller due south, to where in legend the eagles of Zeus found the centre of the world. Here mighty Mount Parnassus looks over the fields and olive groves towards the gulf of Corinth. Parnassus is home to the divine Apollo, who speaks through his prophetess at Delphi. It is in this myth-haunted land, where the road splits into three just before Delphi, that Oedipus (he of the complex) met his father and killed him, unaware of his true identity.

The Delphi road will immediately make clear why it is advisable to take a stout walking staff, and a donkey to carry your luggage. Parnassus is well over a mile high and the road is steep and rocky; so much so that the writer

Pausanias, travelling this way over half a millennium hence, will complain that 'it's rough going, even for a fit and active man'. However, the trip is worth it, for nestled in groves of bay trees on the flanks of the mountain is Delphi, home of the Pythian games, and of the most famous oracle in the known world.

Delphi is always a bustling place, and never more so than when the priestess of Apollo, the Pythia, is about to give her oracular pronouncements. (She does this on the seventh day of the month, but not in winter, when Apollo is away enjoying sunnier climes.) It is not advisable, unless you intend to stay for more than a day, to visit during the Pythian games, as the crowds are unbearable. This does not mean the games are not worth watching. They are a mixture of artistic and sporting events, including musical contests. (You will not see flutes, however. These are usually played at funerals and drinking parties, and are inappropriate for a lively physical event like the games.) There are races that include chariots, and a sprint by men in full armour. But the games add huge crowds to the throng already present, and this makes it difficult to appreciate the beauty, serenity and spectacular views which Delphi has to offer.

The games have taken place every four years since 582 BC, but even when they

Golden over the pediment,
the enchantress sang.

PINDAR • *11TH PAEAN*

The road between Delphi and Tithorea is not mountain all the way. In fact, several of the 25 miles were once said to be suitable for vehicles.

PAUSANIAS • *DESCRIPTION OF GREECE* • 10.5

are not being staged it is worth making your way to the theatre. Here a natural bowl in the hillside can seat thousands of spectators, who can look past the stage and over the breathtaking scenic panorama beyond. Take the winding path to the left of the theatre and ascend to the highest part of Delphi, to the stadium where the athletic events take place. The stadium is built into the slope, with the north section cut into the mountainside and the south section supported by a walled terrace. The track is shaped like a hairpin, and there are small cavities in the stone at one end which the runners use as starting blocks. If anything, the view of the Greek countryside below is even more spectacular.

Spend a few hours wandering among the different treasuries. Every city keeps its own store of treasure at Delphi which they dedicate to Apollo. Cities in desperate financial straits are able to borrow it back – the god does not mind this, as long as it is promptly repaid with interest. This aspect of the strange city of Delphi will later cause it to be irreverently known as 'the Central Reserve Bank of Ancient Greece'. Each city tries to outdo the others with their treasury, not (heaven forbid!) in garish size and grandeur, but in being a gem of architecture in exquisite taste, while delicately hinting that the city that built it could

Typical Delphic treasure house – this is the Siphnian treasury.

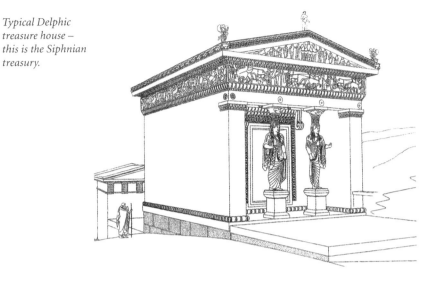

construct a much more lavish monument if it so desired. Naturally, the prime example of this is the Athenian Treasury in the *tenemos* (courtyard) of Apollo. This is a small building in the Doric style (see p. 118), built of Parian marble (a splendid fine-grained, semi-translucent, pure-white marble from the island of Paros). The front and south façade are decorated with lively friezes that mainly feature Theseus, killer of the Minotaur, who is an iconic figure to the Athenians (see p. 32). The walls also serve as a gigantic bulletin board on which the Athenians inscribe honours and dedications. Within are the treasures that they dedicated in thanks for their victory over the Persians. The Oracle rejected the actual spoils captured from the Persians, allegedly because these were brought by Themistokles, the Athenian leader, who later defected to the enemy.

The Athenians, like many Greek citizens and members of Greek colonies beyond the sea, have also put up statues and dedications elsewhere in the precinct. They display the rams from captured enemy ships and bronze shields marked with the offerings from cities under their control – a reminder that Athens is not just a dynamic centre of art and learning, but is also mistress of a considerable empire.

Now step from the Athenian Treasury onto the Sacred Way which runs beside it, and join the supplicants carrying olive branches as they travel to the temple to seek an audience with the Oracle. Consulting the Pythia is not a business to be undertaken lightly. The Oracle is used by cities and even empires to discuss matters of peace or war, so it would be unwise to trouble Apollo with trivial concerns – a brief reading of Greek mythology should reveal the perils of getting an Olympian god personally interested in one's case.

Those determined to visit the Oracle present themselves for consideration with an initial sacrifice called a *pelanos* (this should be bloodless, and hard cash will do nicely). Those accepted to petition Apollo about the future then have to undergo further rites to purify the mind and spirit. When these are completed, they then move up the Sacred Way to stand at the altar of Apollo for a follow-up sacrifice, the *prothysis* (this generally requires a black ram). On regular consultation days the sacrifice is performed by the Delphic authorities on behalf of enquirers, on other days the ritual is performed by the enquirer. Or rather, by the *proxenos*, since foreigners

sacrificing at another city's altars do so indirectly. (The *proxenos* is a tradition whereby each Greek city chooses a citizen in other cities to act as an intermediary between their citizens and the authorities when they visit, roughly the function of a consulate. One of the first things you should do on arriving in Athens is to find the name and address of the *proxenos* who will represent you.)

This second sacrifice needs to go well. The biographer Plutarch, who was himself a priest at Delphi, tells us Apollo will 'return no answer at all, unless the sacrifice trembles all over, even down to its very feet, whilst the wine is poured on its head'. Yet another sacrifice is required within the temple, at the entrance to the Adytum where the consultation will take place. (The Adytum is the sacred part of a temple with access only to authorized personnel – indeed the word *adytum* means 'entry prohibited'.) Enquirers are led individually to their consultation by *prophetai*, who will help to interpret what the god pronounces through his instrument, the Pythia.

Neither is it credible that the Divine Providence should prove to be malevolent only in the matter of divination.

PLUTARCH • *MORALIA* • BK 4

Those expecting to see strange vapours puffing up from a romantic underground cavern whilst a drug-crazed seeress howls nonsense that the worldly-wise interlocutor 'explains' are in for a shock.

Consultation with the Oracle at enquirer's own risk.

Indeed, the enquirer does not see the prophetess at all, as she is in a space below, separated by a barrier – and she is an ordinary woman seated before a very precisely orientated tripod. Earlier in the proceedings she purified herself at the Kastalian spring which flows from the mountain, and burned laurel leaves and barley meal at Apollo's altar. Now, after meditating in the chamber, and holding a sprig of laurel in one hand, she calls out the words and visions which come to her on receiving the enquiry.

If the enquirer himself had a supernatural knowledge of geology, he would speculate on the nature of the hydrocarbon deposits beneath the limestone of Mount Parnassus. The underground activity of the Kastalian spring might release a sweet-smelling gas called ethylene. Inhaling a mild dose of ethylene causes a state of apparent clarity and mild euphoria. This would certainly form a useful conduit to the supernatural if that gas was allowed to build up in an underground chamber, say in the period between consultations.

It happens, sometimes, though not often or at any set time, but as it were, by chance. Those who come for answers from the Oracle find that the room in which they wait is filled with such a fragrant odour and scent that no perfumes in the world can exceed it.

PLUTARCH • *MORALIA* • BK 4

Because the Pythia's visions are sometimes clouded and fragmentary, the interpreter must make of it what he can.

So when Croesus of Lydia (he of the amazing wealth) came to enquire if he should attack the Persians, he was told that a great empire would fall if he did. Sadly, Apollo neglected to mention that the empire that would fall was in fact Croesus' own empire, rather than that of the Persians, but Croesus eventually discovered this for himself. Perhaps the Spartan now awaiting his consultation is among the delegation that, about this time, asked the Oracle if they should go to war with Athens. Apollo replied that if they did go to war he would fight on the Spartan side. And when war breaks out in a year's time, the god will deliver on his promise, shooting arrows of plague to decimate the Athenian population.

Pythian Apollo, master of music, beloved of Olympus and god of prophecy.

Yet the Oracle has also aided the people of Athens, telling them to trust the 'wooden walls' of their triremes which went on to defeat the Persians at the naval battle of Salamis. It also advised them to pray to the winds, and shortly after a mighty storm destroyed much of the Persian fleet.

Perhaps the best advice the traveller can take from Delphi at the start of the onward journey are the two Delphic maxims which have stood the test of time. The first, 'know yourself', was advice allegedly given to Socrates while he was still a young man. The second is 'nothing in excess', which certainly applies to the luggage that the traveller must carry on the difficult road towards the Boeotian plain, and thence overland to Attica. Stop en route if there is time at Mount Helikon, home of the muses and the famous Hippokrene spring, which many later romantic poets will claim as their source of inspiration. If inspired towards romantic adventure, a traveller should note that Boeotian women are as famed for their beauty as Boeotian men are famed for their thick-headedness – but also that even when true, the general is no reliable guide to the particular.

ATTICA

MOUNTS PARNASSUS AND HELIKON belong to the same Parnes range of hills that again confront the traveller at the eastern end of the Boeotian plain. Once through the passes here one is, to all intents and purposes, in Athens.

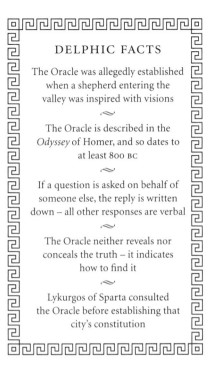

DELPHIC FACTS

The Oracle was allegedly established when a shepherd entering the valley was inspired with visions

~

The Oracle is described in the *Odyssey* of Homer, and so dates to at least 800 BC

~

If a question is asked on behalf of someone else, the reply is written down – all other responses are verbal

~

The Oracle neither reveals nor conceals the truth – it indicates how to find it

~

Lykurgos of Sparta consulted the Oracle before establishing that city's constitution

In fact the road (one of the three main roads that lead into Attica) runs past Panakton, a border fort where young Athenians do garrison duty as part of their military training. Because Attica is a peninsula and the Athenians are secure in their control of the sea, it is only on this northwestern front that Attica needs land defences. The fact that these forts are miles away from the city itself is a reminder that Athens is not only a city, it is also a state, and the land of Attica is where most Athenians live. Despite a lively commercial sector, most Athenians, like all ancient peoples, live outside the city walls. They may go to

THE OX-HOUSE, OR WHEN THE ALPHABET IS ALL GREEK TO YOU

The Greeks willingly admit that they learned the art of writing from the Phoenicians, although they made a few changes of their own. First they added vowels, which Phoenician writing does not have, and then they tidied up the script, in the process tipping many letters on their side. This they could do because the Greek letters were purely representations of sound, whilst the Phoenician were still partly pictograms. For example, 'A' was 'aleph' meaning 'ox', and was depicted by a little horned ox-head. 'B' was 'beth' which means 'house' (as in *bêth lehem*, 'house of bread'), and was depicted by a little two-domed house.

One of the oldest alphabets in the world, Greek will also be one of the most enduring, surviving almost unchanged for the next few millennia into the 21st century. The letters have acquired many symbolic meanings in themselves, such as the mysterious pi (pi = 3·14159) and omega (where the 'alpha and the omega' means the beginning and end of all things). Those finding it all too confusing are advised to head for the nearest bakery and *eta beta pi* to take their minds off it all.

ALPHABET

A	α	alpha
B	β	beta
Γ	γ	gamma
Δ	δ	delta
E	ε	epsilon
Z	ζ	zeta
H	η	eta
Θ	θ	theta
I	ι	iota
K	κ	kappa
Λ	λ	lambda
M	μ	mu
N	ν	nu
Ξ	ξ	xi
O	o	omicron
Π	π	pi
P	ρ	rho
Σ	σ	sigma
T	τ	tau
Y	υ	upsilon
Φ	φ	phi
X	χ	chi
Ψ	ψ	psi
Ω	ω	omega

Athens to vote, or to buy goods not available in the local markets, and they certainly go there for the big festivals, but for many 'Athenians' their home is their 'deme' or local community in which they are registered. Athens has about 140 such demes, with populations varying from about 100 to several thousand, spread over the 930 square miles of Attica.

The Athenians identify themselves by their highly extended family groups ('phratries') which are often dominated by particular clans ('genes'), and by their demes. Membership of a deme is essential for Athenian citizens, and even forms part of their names, so an Athenian might introduce himself as, for example, Kleon of Araphen, son of

Hipparchos. Athenians also belong to one of ten tribes, each named after a mythological hero, but this is no ancient lineage. This is part of the same political reform of 508 BC which organized the demes into their present form.

Attica is a land of villages and towns. Most people live within a community, and individual farmhouses are rare. It is not unusual for a well-off Athenian family to own several fragmented patches of land, and these keep changing according to marriage, death and financial well-being, but this land is almost invariably within the family's own deme. Nor are these demes simply political units – members of each one have their own particular character and outlook.

Anyone having business within a particular deme might find things easier if the help of the 'demarch' is enlisted. This is an elected official who performs the functions of a mayor, supervising the important activities of the deme, registering young men as they come of age, and determining who is eligible to vote in the assembly. He (every Greek in public life is male) is always an important and well-connected member of the community, and a man whose friendship is definitely worth cultivating.

The Ikarians and the deme of the Ikarians crown Nikon the demarch for conducting the festival and games in honour of Dionysos in a proper manner.

INSCRIPTION FROM IKARIA
DISCOVERED IN 1888

Unlike the cosmopolitan city itself, inland Attica is parochial and less used to strangers. The dry, low-lying land is not ideal for agriculture. In fact the ridge of rock which forms the Parnes hills continues to disrupt the terrain, and will remain a feature of the landscape all the way to the lofty pyramid of Mount Pentelikus, overlooking the plain of Marathon. Because of the thin rocky soil, many in the countryside follow other occupations, such as charcoal-burning, quarrying and tanning leather. Beekeeping is a common occupation, and the Athenians are also intensely proud of the quality of their olives. Indeed, they claim the tree originated in Attica. There is a legend that when Poseidon and Athena competed to become the patron god of Athens, the men voted for Poseidon but were out-voted by the women. They chose Athena, who bestowed their land with the olive.

Athens often needs to import wheat, usually from colonies on the Black Sea which do a much better job of growing it. Nevertheless, agriculture is an idealized occupation, and every Athenian would like to be a landowner. Fortunately, the quality of farmland is as

Some old dotards from Acharnae, rough and ruthless ... veterans of Marathon, and tough as oak or maple, and certainly made from the same.

ARISTOPHANES
ACHARNIANS • 180–81

varied as the Attic countryside itself, and a field can be purchased for anywhere between ten and 500 drachmas, depending on its size and quality.

There are few grassy plains in Attica, and consequently few cattle, but sheep and goats wander about the scrub on the sides of the road, or in fields left to lie fallow. One also often comes across small herds of pigs rooting around in groves of trees, or sprawling in pens at the back of homesteads. Oranges are unknown at this time, but the vineyards on the sunny slopes produce some of the best wine in the Greek world.

Figs grow well in Attica, but only in selected areas. To prevent these areas being bought up by the rich and the figs shipped abroad, Solon – an early legislator – forbade the export from Greece of Athenian dried figs, thus making sure that figs were available for the general population. Reporting on illegal fig-smuggling rapidly became a way of currying favour with the authorities. So much so that a being a sycophant (a 'fig tell-tale') has for evermore described one who sucks up to those in power.

On the roads of Attica you will often come across herms, representations of Hermes, the god of travel and trade – for example there is one positioned on the road exactly between each deme and Athens itself. These statues are topped by a bust of the god whilst the rectangular block of the main body is punctuated by the exclamation mark of a startlingly erect penis (symbolizing good fortune and abundance). Beneath this is an injunction along the lines of: 'Go your way, thinking proper thoughts.'

The roads are busy with traffic, most of it carts and pedestrians. Market gardeners bring their vegetable produce to the city, and tradesmen and merchants make their way to the individual mar-

> *I'd had a lovely time up to that point, a crude, uncomplicated, country life, lying around just as I pleased, with honey bees, and sheep and olives.*
>
> STREPSIADES IN
> ARISTOPHANES
> *THE CLOUDS* • 53

A farmer at the plough while his wife scatters seeds behind him.

Profile of a herm clearly showing its outstanding features.

demes, which have a busy cultural, economic and religious life of their own. At certain times of the year, as many people may be going to cult centres at Sounion, Rhamnos or Eleusis as to Athens itself.

To experience life in the demes, one should consider Rhamnos, nestling in a small sheltered bay just north of Marathon. The temple and sanctuary at Rhamnos, situated just past the necropolis to the north of the deme, are well worth the visit. This is particularly true if you have any business with the resident goddess, Nemesis, who distributes divine retribution on wrongdoers, especially the overly proud and arrogant. Admire particularly the statue of the goddess by the sculptor Agorakritos. It was made from a magnificent block of Parian marble that the Persians brought along during their invasion, confidently expecting to carve it into a monument commemorating their conquest of Athens.

There is a splendid view of the bay from the sanctuary, which will be particularly relished by those enjoying new-found peace of mind after having appeased the vengeance of the goddess. Rhamnos is also useful for those needing to get to Attica in a hurry, as there is a small port dealing mainly with the import of grain from the nearby island of Euboea. The gymnasium, theatre and acropolis of Rhamnos testify to the fact that Athenian citizens can enjoy rich and fulfilling lives without setting foot in the city itself.

kets in the demes. Ordinary Athenians visit the city for business or pleasure remarkably frequently, and think little of walking a round trip of 20 miles or so in the process. While some wear sandals for the journey, many are barefoot. Barefoot is the usual condition indoors, and some men go their entire lives with nothing on their feet (although some of the nearer demes, acknowledging that many of their members actually live in the city rather than the deme itself, regularly hold their meetings in Athens and thus save their members a bit of walking). Other Athenians travel between the

MARATHON

SEVEN-AND-A-HALF-MILES TO THE southwest of Rhamnos lies another little deme, tucked into a patch of flat ground near Mount Agrieliki. Here the ground is well-watered, and vegetables are grown for sale in the markets of Athens, some two score miles distant. There is little in this small, quiet market town to suggest that, a generation ago, the future of western civilization hinged on what was happening here.

Yet wander south for a mile or so towards the main road from Athens, where Agrieliki comes closer to the sea and the sanctuary of Herakles sits close against the road. Now you stand where the Athenian troops – armoured warriors called hoplites after their large round shields (*hoploi*) – mustered to confront a massive Persian army which threatened to overwhelm their city and stamp out the torch of cultural and political innovation in Athens before it was fully lit.

The Persians were formed up eight stades away. The bowmen fitted arrows to their bows, confident of mowing down the Greek hoplites before they could reach the Persian lines. What they did not expect was that as they fired, the Athenians would break into a furious sprint. (This is where all those races in full armour at sporting events paid off.) The volley of arrows whizzed over the heads of the charging Greeks, who then ploughed into the front ranks of the lightly armoured Persian army.

It is easy to see where this happened, for in the middle of the plain of Marathon there stands a huge mound of earth (a *soros*) where the 192 Athenian casualties lie. Usually burials of war dead take place in the city, but these heroes were honoured by being interred where they fell, and their monument, almost 160 feet across and 30 feet high, is unmissable from almost anywhere on the plain.

On the flank of the battle line, where the tide of battle turned in favour of the Athenians, stands the victory memorial, the Trope, a tall and handsome marble column. Not far beyond lies a long shallow ditch into which the bodies of the slain Persians – over 6,000 of them – were unceremoniously tumbled. There is also a separate grave for Miltiades, the Athenian leader, who died later but asked that he be interred at the site of his great victory.

Miltiades erected me, goat-footed Pan, the Arcadian, enemy of the Medes, friend of the Athenians.

DEDICATION TO PAN
AT MARATHON

Anyone wanting a souvenir of the battle need only cross the river Charada, and look in the wide marsh beyond. The Persians were driven into this marsh in their thousands by the victorious Athenians, and those who did not escape to their ships died there. Sporting males might decide to strip off and run the distance from Marathon to Athens in emulation of the feat of Pheidippides, who brought the news of victory to the city (though Pheidippides died from his exertions, so too close emulation is to be avoided). Note that in Athens, unlike Sparta, women most emphatically do not exercise in the nude.

Those wanting to reach Athens in a more conventional fashion should charter one of the fishing boats that frequent the bay, and enjoy a sail to the *polis* round Cape Sounion, admiring en route the magnificent temple of Poseidon under construction on the headland.

II · THE PIRAEUS

The Harbours § Piraean People
The Long Walls

THE HARBOURS

THE HILLY PENINSULA OF THE Piraeus is part of the *chora*, the territory of Athens, rather than part of the city itself. It is yet another deme, albeit a large one with a decidedly unique character. The Piraeus came relatively recently into its role as the main port of Athens – until the Persian wars the wide, open bay of Phaleron just to the east did the job. However, as the warlike triremes thronging the outer part of the main harbour testify, Athens is now a major naval power, and needs harbour facilities to match. Maritime power has also introduced the Athenians to the joys of maritime trade, so that the Piraeus is now the gateway through which products from all over the world are channelled to markets in Athens and Attica. Consequently the Piraeus has grown in size and population, and now rivals the main city of Athens itself.

The main harbour at the Piraeus is Kantharos, with the small, almost circular harbours of Zea and Munychia to the east, on the other side of the peninsula. On entering Kantharos, look

> *Good things from all over the world flow into our city, so it is just as natural for us to enjoy foreign goods as local produce.*
>
> PERIKLES IN THUCYDIDES
> *HISTORY OF THE*
> *PELOPONNESIAN WAR* · 2.38

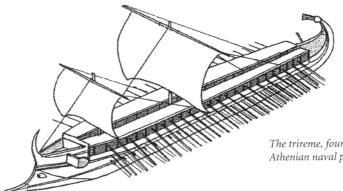

The trireme, foundation of Athenian naval power.

for a plain white marble column on the headland to the right. This is said to mark the tomb of Themistokles, mastermind of the war against the Persians, who later defected to the enemy. It is whispered that after his death his bones were secretly restored to his homeland and interred here. (The Athenian authorities carefully avoid checking to see if this is so.) When they sight this column, most traders make a quick assessment of their position relative to other ships approaching the harbour, as this is now the time for a quick sprint to secure the best possible berth. For most this means passing the ship-sheds in the outer harbour and seeking a dock in the inner, commercial harbour, particularly a place on the wharves of the emporium on the eastern side. Five large porticoes stand nearby, serving both as storage for goods from Egypt, Persia, Syracuse and other exotic locations, and as offices for the traders who deal with them.

Everything, dishes of salt fish, wine, tapestries, cheese, honey, sesame-fruit, cushions, flagons, rich clothing, chaplets, necklets, drinking-cups, all that yields pleasure and health.

BDELYKLEON IN ARISTOPHANES
THE WASPS • 676–77

These wharves are also where passengers take a ferry to Aegina, 18 miles away across the Saronic gulf. It is worth paying the two obols fare for a quick excursion to the island and town of the same name, especially to see the splendid temple of Aphaea. This building completes

Weighing merchandise at the docks. Athens is a major centre of trade.

an equilateral triangle of temples, with the Parthenon and the temple of Poseidon at Sounion at the other corners. Alternatively, take a ferry to Salamis and cross the waters of the strait, where, after Marathon and Thermopylae, the decisive battle against the Persians was fought at sea.

Trade is the Piraeus' *raison d'etre*. The industrious citizens of the deme ensure that Athenians enjoy corn and dried fish from the Euxine (an area of the Black Sea), cheeses from Sicily, exotic spices and silks from the Orient and slippers from Persia. Timber – which does not grow well in Athens – is imported from Crete, Africa and Syria. This is not the only product imported for the Athenian building boom – look for large, wide-bodied boats parked with a few yards between them. Heavy timber beams laid between the boats keep the distance fixed, and from the beams are suspended marble column drums. These are about five tons apiece, but are kept totally underwater to reduce their displacement. They are the columns that will eventually end up in the stoas and temples of the city. Other ships are unloading luxury goods. Over the years, imported dyes and fabrics have allowed men's clothing – and even more so, women's clothing – to develop a range of exotic colours, and hemlines are now often richly patterned or decorated with motifs. Most of these goods are transported to the main market of Athens, the Agora, but there is also a lively trade at the harbour as merchants strive to cut out their rivals by dealing directly with newcomers as they dock.

Kantharos shows the Piraeus as a centre of commerce. But leave behind the warehouses and trading offices at the docks, and make your way inland to the east. For 500 yards or so you pass through busy streets, echoing with the clang of metalwork from the small workshops, and redolent with the smell of tanning leather, baking bread and the reek of too many people with too few sewage facilities. When you have crossed through to the other side of the peninsula, the naked power of imperial Athens is on display at Zea, the main harbour of the Athenian navy. The triremes thronging the entrance of

Kantharos may have been impressive, but there are berths for another 196 ships at Zea, and behind these is the menacing bulk of the huge arsenal where weapons and ships' rigging are stored. It is impossible to get too close to all this as the area is walled off, and a special pass is needed to get by the sentries at the gates.

I see a man emptying his bowels in the Piraeus, close to the house where the bad girls are.
TRYGAEUS IN ARISTOPHANES
PEACE • 185–88

The Piraeus has had the benefit of urban planning by the great city architect Hippodamos of Miletos, and to him the deme owes its regular block pattern of streets, and the magnificent, crowd-thronged agora beside the arsenal. Whilst at Zea, visit the law court in Phreatto, right beside the sea. Here you might catch some decidedly odd legal proceedings under way. This court deals with the cases of those who have been exiled from Athens. Exiles make their appeal for return to the judges – from a boat moored just offshore.

The Piraeus is not just about trade and war. It has its own theatre, and a sanctuary to Artemis on a hill near Munychia, the third harbour (also for warships but used by some local shipping). The area is well stocked with temples, since making one's living amid the risks of seaborne trade is conducive to a religious disposition. Those with a taste for eclectic worship will find that the cosmopolitan population of the Piraeus caters for almost every preference. Amongst others there are shrines to Bendis from Thrace, Isis of Egypt, and Baal of Phoenicia.

PIRAEAN PEOPLE

FOR ALL ITS RELATIVE NEWNESS, the Piraeus has a bustling, hard-edged feel, and not a little squalor. Prostitutes line the quayside, offering sailors a traditional greeting, and, in the words of one offended trader, 'debilitating the workers hired to unload the corn'. Some of the most despised Athenian social classes make their home in the Piraeus. Those unloading the corn may be slaves – in fact most are – but free men in desperate need of money will take on the work. It involves swallowing their pride to do so, for Athenians feel it utterly debasing for a free man to have an employer other than himself. This 'every man his own master' attitude means that the Piraeus is home to many one-man businesses, mainly craft shops, with a single self-employed artisan and his family engaged in working metal, ceramic or leather. Large-scale manufacturing hardly exists. Because of the expansion of the fleet and the huge building programme currently under way in the city, many artisans are engaged on state contracts – much to the annoyance of Athenians who are finding it hard to get a good plumber or someone to fit a new door in the house.

Do you not see what scores of carpenters and house-builders there are who spend their time in building houses for half the world; but for themselves they simply cannot do it, and are forced to live in lodgings.

XENOPHON • SYMPOSIUM • 4

One step socially above the craftsmen are the traders, a breed whom Athenians instinctively distrust. If a man does not directly produce something, but simply moves it from the possession of one person to another, how does the trader make money if not by cheating one or the other party of fair value? These traders are often metics, or resident aliens.

The Athenians reserve citizenship of their city for those who are native-born, holding themselves to be an autochthonous breed – literally 'sprung by themselves from the earth'. More precisely, the men come from a patch of earth impregnated by semen which Athena wiped away from her leg as an unwanted and premature offering from the somewhat over-excited god Hephaestos. Athenian women, on the other hand, are descended from Pandora, the first woman (she of Pandora's box).

Since the Athenians regard being Athenian as a hereditary condition, those born of non-Athenian parents can no more be Athenian than dogs can be cats. Consequently metics may be born in Athens, and be Athenian in religion, outlook and culture, but they are not Athenian. Alternatively, they may be Phoenicians, Corinthians or Egyptians who have been in residence less than six months – or anything in

PERI ATHENON

The ship sheds in Kantharos are
capable of sheltering
almost 100 warships

~

Ship sheds are needed because
triremes are not very seaworthy, and
have to be parked for the winter

~

By far the largest 'factory' in Athens is
engaged in making shields, and this employs only about 100 slaves

~

There is a quarry just within the northwestern wall of the Piraeus, from which
came much of the stone for the walls

~

The Piraeus has been inhabited
since *c.* 2500 BC

~

In prehistoric times the Piraeus
was an island

~

Kantharos is one of the largest natural
harbours in the Mediterranean

Despite being close to Athens,
Aegina has not always been friendly
with that city, causing Perikles to call
Aegina 'the eyesore of the Piraeus'

~

Sea trade is usually carried out
by a trader (*emperos*) who rents or leases
either cargo space or an entire ship from
a ship-owner (*naukleros*)

~

Kantharos means 'vase',
and the port gets its name from
the harbour's shape

~

Zea, the second largest
harbour of the Piraeus, is about
500 yards across

~

Even when not wearing trousers,
barbarians are recognized by the
oafish speech which gives them their
name. Unlike the liquid fluency of
Greek, their language, with its harsh
bar-bar sounds, jars on the ear

between. Every metic needs to have a citizen sponsor, who acts for him as a sort
of personal *proxenos* in dealings with
authority. Metics also have a special tax
levied on them for the privilege of living
in Athens, and are liable to enslavement
if they fail to pay. Although metics may
be honoured with the privileges of citizens for exceptional services, most are
seen by Athenians as a lower class of person – as is reflected by the fact that the
punishment for murdering a metic is
milder than that for slaying a citizen.

Despite these drawbacks, Athens has
a huge foreign population who find the
vibrancy of intellectual and economic
life in Athens irresistible. In the Piraeus
there are considerably more metics than
Athenians, and their presence helps to
make Piraeus a more lively, tolerant and
cosmopolitan place than the main city
four miles to the northeast.

Women Even before one reaches the main city, it becomes plain that male chauvinism is rampant in Athens.

I praise my good fortune in being born a man and not a beast, a Greek and not a barbarian, and a man and not a woman.

THALES OF MILETUS • 585 BC

A woman's sphere is in the private realm of the house, supervising the slaves, caring for the children, cooking and weaving cloth. (Weaving cloth is a perpetual occupation for all classes of Athenian women. The Archon's wife does it while her husband presides over the jury court, and prostitutes do it during slack times at the brothel. Girls learn to weave and spin wool at an early age – in fact the sacred robe of Athena is made by citizen girls, and the goddess is given a

It is the glory of a woman not to be mentioned, whether in praise or in blame.

PERIKLES IN THUCYDIDES
*HISTORY OF THE
PELOPONNESIAN WAR* • 2.45

new one every year.) Women can't vote or even attend the assembly, and in legal disputes they are represented by fathers or guardians. It is a disgrace for a woman to have to appear in court for any reason at all.

Later Athenians will feel a mixture of shock and bemusement the occasion when the (in)famous *hetaera* Phryne is charged with impiety. As a courtesan, Phryne has many lovers, including Hypereides, her defender and advocate. She herself only appears in court when it is clear that words alone are not going to sway the jury. Hypereides strips off her tunic and bares her breasts, arguing that one could hardly condemn for impiety one who was so evidently 'Aphrodite's representative'. The jury are overwhelmed by 'religious awe' and vote for her acquittal.

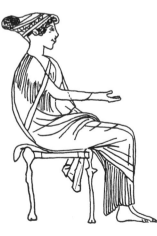

Athenian mother and child, a popular theme on vase paintings.

Weaving is the constant occupation of Athenian women.

Phryne herself shows how women generally manage to subvert the wishful thinking of the average Athenian male, who tries to typecast women as either respectable citizen ladies (with whom any male indulging in sex outside marriage may be arbitrarily killed by the husband or father), or as low-life slatterns who have no morals at all. In fact, Athenian women generally manage to enforce their views in private (on visiting Socrates later we will discover he is hen-pecked), or prevail upon a male to enforce their views for them in public.

As the economy could not function without women in work, they are, in every sense, more visible in the Piraeus. The perfect Athenian housewife from Attica or the main city is practically a walking tent when in public, dressed from head to foot in her *peplos* (a sort of blanket held on with pins), and generally with a shawl over her head for good measure. But even then it is rare that this paragon be seen in public, and certainly not in free-wheeling Piraeus where bare-armed working-class lasses cheerfully gut fish, swap ribald badinage and serve in market stalls, whilst the prostitutes are blatant about what they have to offer.

Slaves Among the items presented for sale on the wharves of the emporium are human beings. Athenians, like all Greeks, regard slavery as a fundamental fact of existence. In fact, in a century's time Aristotle will define the Greek nuclear family as 'a man, his wife and their slave'. Naturally, Aristotle was not including the Athenian poor in his description, and ignoring the fact that many small-holdings in Attica are worked by free-born labour, but even in the more egalitarian Piraeus about a quarter of the population are slaves. Since slaves dress in a very similar way to other Athenians it is hard to tell a slave from, for example, a *thete*, the lowest class of Athenian citizen. One distinguishing feature is that slaves often sport tattoos, either relics of their barbarian past (some Thracian slaves have very elegant tattoos on their necks), or as marks by their owners indicating that a particular slave is untrustworthy or likely to run away.

Life as an Athenian slave depends a lot on the individual slave's background. Greeks are somewhat uneasy about enslaving fellow Greeks, although they do it often enough. However, Greeks are the type of slave most often emancipated, or given cushy jobs in the city

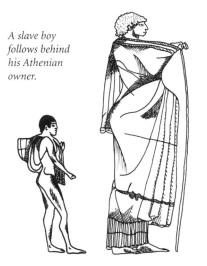

A slave boy follows behind his Athenian owner.

since a slave-owning Athenian woman does not venture out to do her own shopping. This relationship between owners and owned can lead to tension, but also to camaraderie and even love.

Far worse are the fates of barbarians whom one sees herded out to labour in the fields of the wealthy, or the unfortunates sold to brothels (this can also happen to men, but is a more common fate for women). Some household slaves prefer suicide to this option, and in one recent case a girl who heard she was to be sold to a brothel took the chance to poison her former master with the last meal she cooked for him. Just as women fear the brothel, male slaves dread being sent to the mines. Silver is the backbone of the finances of imperial Athens, so her empire is built on the backs of those slaves who suffer and die in the mines at Laurium, well out of sight of the philosophers in the Agora.

administration. Barbarians, on the other hand, are natural-born slaves, because, well, they are *barbarians*, and self-evidently incapable of benefiting from being anything better.

The *demesioi* are the upper echelon of slavery. Athens employs several hundred of these, in roles such as official coin-testers in the markets, or clerks in the law courts. State slaves also serve as the rough equivalent of the city watch, with a number of bow-carrying Skythians amongst them. In the Piraeus there are slaves who are skilled craftsmen. They live in their own workshops and are hardly distinguishable from free men, apart from when the master comes around to collect his substantial cut of the earnings. Household slaves do the menial tasks, and often learn a trade by assisting in their master's work. They are frequently encountered in the market,

THE LONG WALLS

ATHENS RELIES ON THE SEA more than she relies on Attica, and while the countryside may be devastated by invading armies, the Piraeus must be protected at all costs. Unlike the walls of Athens itself, the walls of the Piraeus were not built in a frantic hurry. Behind this 'frantic hurry' with which the walls of Athens were built, there lies a tale. The Persians had thrown down the old walls of Athens, and after they had been kicked out of Greece the Spartans made a friendly suggestion that Athens did not need walls, as they could rely on the Spartans to defend them. This 'friendly suggestion' from a powerful state with a ferocious army was enough to galvanize the entire population of Athens – men, women and children – into becoming high-speed wall builders. In their haste, they used whatever material came to hand. If the masonry looked suitable, says the historian Thucydides, 'no private or public building was spared'.

The wily Themistokles, who was still popular with the Athenians at this point, went to Sparta to stop them interfering with the rebuilding. His argument was roughly: 'Walls? Someone reported walls? Nonsense. Oh, those walls. We'll talk about it (much) later. All right. We have walls. Big, strong safe ones. Want to make something of it?'

He [Themistokles] kneaded the Piraeus into a cake for her [Athens] to eat for lunch.

ARISTOPHANES • THE
KNIGHTS • 185–86

Even now it can be seen that the city walls were a rushed job. The foundations are made of different sorts of stone, sometimes not even carved to fit, but simply jammed in wherever the shape was most appropriate. Pillars from old tombs nestle against inscriptions, fragments of sculpture and dismantled sections of houses. These walls tell us much about the Athenians, their civic pride, and their whole-hearted commitment to something once they have decided to get it, whatever the cost.

As a Corinthian ambassador once complained, 'If the Athenians want something and don't get it, they act as though it has been taken away from them. If they do get it, they regard it as the basis of the next thing they want ... their idea of a holiday is to do something positive, preferring hardship and activity to peace and quiet. They are naturally incapable of living a quiet life, or of letting anyone else have one.'

Even the walls of the Piraeus are only half the height that they were originally intended to be. However, these walls were built at a more leisurely pace and are still remarkably imposing, since more time available meant that more care was taken in the building. All around the seven-and-a-half mile circuit of the harbour walls there is space for two waggons to pass each other along the wide top. With a normal fortification the space between the inner and outer wall is filled with clay or rubble, but the Piraeus wall has large blocks of stone which were lowered into the gap, and then held in place with iron or lead clamps. There are regular towers along the walls – round towers that were a part of Themistokles' original design, and rectangular ones added later.

WHAT'S THAT WALL?

The speed with which the Athenian walls were built meant that each builder could go with the style that suited him best, depending on the materials available. Opposite are a few to look for.

Leaving the Piraeus to go to Athens proper does not entail leaving the shelter of the city walls. The present government, led by Perikles, has worked hard and at huge expense to connect the whole four-and-a-half mile distance with formidable walls, running parallel about 200 yards apart, with a wide road between them and a massive protective gate at either end. These defences are even later and built more thoroughly than the other walls, and are of large, well-shaped masonry blocks, generally polyagonal or isodomic, and so new that the marks of the mason's chisels are still unweathered. There was a bit of tricky engineering to be done where the river Kephisos flows across the Attic plain to Phaleron bay, entering the sea near Munychia. The walls have to cross this river about a mile-and-a-half out of the Piraeus, and though the river is not wide, the banks are very boggy. (The marshy ground to the southwest is impossible to build on and is used as a cemetery.) The outer, west-facing wall is garrisoned, with the shapes of hoplites in their armour silhouetted against the sky.

The inner wall has no garrison at present, for to reach this wall an invader would have to attack from the east, and must first get past the single wall which leads from Athens to Phaleron. The intervening plain between the walls is well-watered and farmed, for in the event of Athens coming under siege, the market gardens here provide valuable fresh fruit and vegetables. The space between the Long Walls also provides a handy camping ground if the populace of Attica are driven from their homes by an overwhelming enemy force.

Isodomic • regular stone blocks laid like bricks, though these bricks might weigh hundreds of pounds each. Used when there is time and money to spare.

Pseudo-Isodomic • cheating slightly by alternating smaller, cheaper layers of flat stone with the more expensive blocks.

Polyagonal • when irregular blocks of stone are brought to the wall, and carved to fit on the spot. Many of the walls of Athens have this form.

Rubble • for quick cheap walls in a hurry. Stones are roughly carved, jammed together and mortar is slapped over the resulting heap.

Trapezoidal • an experimental technique where the stone 'bricks' are alternately wider at the top and the bottom, making the wall more resistant to lateral shocks.

III · ORIENTATION

Getting About § Where to Stay
Athenian Society

Tell me, in case I should need them, all about the hosts who received you, tell me of them as well as of the harbours, the bakeries, the brothels, the drinking-shops, the fountains, the roads, the eating-houses and of the hostels where there are the fewest bugs.

DIONYSOS IN ARISTOPHANES
THE FROGS · 133–39

ANYONE LOST IN ATHENS SHOULD call to mind the verse from a Hebrew sacred text. Lift up thine eyes to the hills, for there certainly help is to be found. Standing 300 feet higher than most of the city, the rocky crag of the Acropolis dominates the physical aspect of Athens just as its ideological significance dominates the psyche of its citizens.

The Acropolis was the original core of Athens, and still today it is the spiritual home of the Athenians and their fortress of last resort. The Acropolis is a flat-topped rocky outcrop, roughly tear-shaped along an east–west axis, with the uniquely beautiful Parthenon at the top on the central south side. A quick glance at the Parthenon relative to your position is therefore enough to give you your bearings wherever you are in the city.

Those in the northeast of Athens will see the crooked pointy witch's hat of Mount Lykabettos sticking up over the

the city walls. Legend says this hill was dropped here, about a mile from the city, as discarded building material by Athena whilst the goddess was constructing the Acropolis.

If Mount Lykabettos is on the left as you look at the Acropolis, then you are in the north of the city facing south. From here, especially if Boreas the north wind is blowing, native Athenians can navigate blindfolded by calibrating the smell from the river Eridanos. This small river runs from east to west across the north section of Athens, becoming proportionately more sullied by its experience of urban life as it goes along. By the time it flows past the Agora and out of the city by the Kerameikos gate, the stench has reached legendary proportions.

Athens expanded from the original settlement around the Acropolis, and stopped more or less at the point where the local infrastructure could not support many more people. The walls mark the limit of this expansion, and seen from above they resemble a very rough oval, with a notable bulge on the oval's top (north) side. This shape means that if you are in the city you are within a mile of the Acropolis, which makes it essentially unmissable.

GETTING ABOUT

THE ATHENIANS DON'T GIVE NAMES to their streets, which means that every address comes more or less complete with a description of how to get there. For example, Philokrates of Hagnous has his house in Melite on the south side of the road leading from the shrine of Herakles. Since Athens is littered with shrines, these are handy navigational guides. It would help if the speaker was more specific about which of the dozens of shrines to Herakles he is referring to – in this case 'Herakles the evil-averter'.

Some cities like to have a 'sacred agora' where all the shrines are placed together, and one can compare the competition before making an offering to the deity of choice.

Property of Diodorus, a house in Kydathenaion with a porch and two pillars, adjacent to the shrine of Artemis.

5TH-CENTURY PROPERTY DESCRIPTION • *HESPERIA 22 STELE 6 • 78-79*

Athens, however, has shrines, houses, workshops, theatres and law courts all jumbled together. Many temples stand beside domestic dwellings, so it is not uncommon to have a god for a neighbour.

Sometimes, instead of a shrine, the landmark might be a *heroon*, a sort of monument to the memory of a mythological hero – Theseus for example. Other navigation points include herms and 'hekatons', representations of Hekate, the goddess who guards the crossroads or where three roads meet. Her distinctive, multiple-bodied statue is often used to point travellers in the right direction. Getting to an address involves a few of these waypoints, so a traveller may be told: 'At the hekaton near the workshop of Kalliandros take the road to the Areopagus, stop by the well near the shrine to Apollo, and the right hand hekaton faces the street where Kallista lives. Look for a house where the herm out in front has a chipped base.'

As in every ancient city, workmen in the same trades tend to cluster in the same area, making it easier to pop next door and borrow a chisel or a cup of granite chippings. It also means that some streets have nicknames – the street of the swordsmiths, or the street of the herm-makers. Pot-makers are so common that a whole area in the northwest is named after them – the Kerameikon – although the area of the Kerameikon outside the walls is a cemetery.

Like the rest of Attica, Athens is divided into demes. There is populous Kydathenaion in the north, and Kollytos and Melite in the south and west. The other city demes are Skambonidai and Koile. The water courses of the city also help with navigation. We have already, to our regret, met the Eridanos. Its equivalent on the Piraeus side is a huge drain, which is fortunately covered over at times, and in the south side of the city people also have the aqueduct, constructed a century ago, which supplements the water supply from the wells.

THESEUS FACT-FILE

(Since Athenians revere Theseus, and he keeps popping up in different contexts,
it is worth knowing a bit about this tainted Athenian hero)

≈

He is descended on his mother's side from Pelops, after whom the Peloponnese is named

≈

He was a famous killer of savage beasts and bandits while still a young man

≈

He volunteered to be part of the tribute to king Minos, who regularly sacrificed
seven Athenian youths and virgins in a labyrinth

≈

The killing was done by Minos' step-son, the half-man, half-bull Minotaur

≈

Finding his way through the maze with a thread given by the beautiful and
love-struck Ariadne, Theseus killed the Minotaur and escaped

≈

On his return he became king of Athens, and united Attica under the leadership of the city

≈

He abducted and married an Amazon, and had to fight the rest of that nation
when they invaded Athens

≈

When he was 50 he was arrested for abducting an under-age girl from
a neighbouring state

≈

Although later released, he could not repair his reputation in Athens and he was
deposed. He fled to the island of Skyros, where he was assassinated

≈

A generation ago, his body was 'found' on Skyros and brought back to Athens

*Theseus slays
the Minotaur.*

I *Athena Parthenos in her serene majesty. As always, she sports her helmet and shield, but here she has set aside her spear and instead holds Victory in her outstretched hand. While this gold and ivory statue within the Parthenon is the most famous depiction of Athena, statues and images of the goddess are plentiful in the city.*

II *Athens as seen by the eagles of Apollo, approaching from the northwest. The tightly packed houses within the city walls are in contrast with the khaki and olive-green countryside of Attica, and the Acropolis and Parthenon are instantly recognizable landmarks.*

III *The Acropolis during the Panathenaia. The Athenians pour through the Propylaea where the little shrine of Athena Nike looks down on them from the right, and on entering the Acropolis the celebrants see before them the Erechtheion to the left, and the impressive frontage of the Parthenon to the right.*

IV *A view across the Agora from the Acropolis showing the Panathenaic Way as it runs past the Altar of the Twelve Gods, the Stoa of Zeus Eleuthereos and the Royal Stoa, with the Painted Stoa on the right. The road then sweeps on towards the Dipylon and Sacred gates in the distance. On the hill in the background is the temple of Hephaestos.*

V *The southwest corner of the Agora, showing the distinctive 'sun-hat' of the Tholos and the unique diamond-shaped tiles of its roof. The Bouleuterion stands beside this building, and the temple of Hephaestos is again in the background.*

VI *This closer look at the Acropolis shows why the hill is not just a temple complex, but also a formidable fortress. The sheer slopes allow access only through the ramp leading to the Propylaea, and it was on this hill that the defenders of Athens made a doomed last stand against the Persians just 50 years ago. The Persians destroyed the temples of the Acropolis, which have now been rebuilt even more gloriously than before.*

LEFT An armourer polishes off another helmet.

RIGHT A craftsman gives the finishing touches to a herm.

In Athens, as a general rule, walking along any major thoroughfare will lead either to a city gate or to the Agora, which lies just to the northwest of the Acropolis. For example the Processional Way runs from by the Dipylon gate to the top of the Acropolis – via the Agora. Other major roads lead from the Agora to the Acharnian gate in the northeast, and another winds through the busy workshops along the valley between the Acropolis and the hill of the Nymphs towards the Piraeus gate in the west.

WHERE TO STAY

VISITORS TO ATHENS COME FOR a variety of reasons. Their purposes may be diplomatic, religious, social, family or business, or a combination of these factors, since, for example, it is a poor diplomat who does not do any socializing during his visit. However, travel is still a tricky business in 5th-century Greece, so facilities for tourists simply do not exist. There are *lesche*, which are a sort of club-house for those without other facilities in the city, but they do not offer overnight accommodation. (In Athens there is one in the 'art-gallery' of the Propylaea, p. 117.) Ambassadors have special quarters put aside by the city for their use, and many religious shrines provide accommodation for pilgrims. While the quality of the religious lodgings can be far from divine, even the worst of them are probably superior to the common inns.

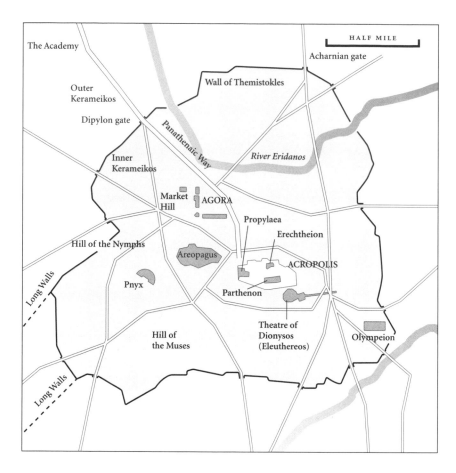

The Academy

HALF MILE

Acharnian gate

Wall of Themistokles

Outer
Kerameikos

Dipylon gate

Panathenaic Way

Inner
Kerameikos

River Eridanos

Market
Hill   AGORA

Propylaea

Erechtheion

Hill of the Nymphs

Areopagus

ACROPOLIS

Long Walls

Pnyx

Parthenon

Hill of
the Muses

Theatre of
Dionysos
(Eleuthereos)

Olympeion

Long Walls

These are notorious for larcenous land-lords, ravenous bed-bugs, insistent and slatternly prostitutes, and violent drunks who may or may not be pimping the prostitutes in question.

By far the best bet is to try to find through your personal connections an Athenian who is willing to provide you with accommodation because he wishes to establish a contact with someone from your city. Like all Greeks, the Athenians are enormously hospitable and welcoming to travellers, perhaps because so many legends tell of the grue-some end, or positive rewards, that fol-low the treatment of a deity who stops by incognito for his or her own nefari-ous purposes.

Or perhaps it is simply that the pres-ence of a stranger enlivens gatherings with news of the outside world, and pro-vides contact with the exotic which is so relished by the inquiring and lively Athenian mind. *Xenia* is the Greek term for hospitality, and it embeds within it a set of social conventions. The guest is expected to attempt as far as possible to minimize the inconvenience of his presence, and to repay hospitality as far as is possible with stories, or if so talented, with songs or poetry.

On one famous occasion, the tyrant Kleisthenes invited a young Athenian to dinner who he was considering as a spouse for his daughter. During the after-dinner festivities, the lad demonstrated a talent for dancing, which he chose to do on the table (including some uninhibited break-dancing on his head, which revealed an unfortunate lack of underwear). The reproving Kleisthenes sternly told the gathering, 'Hippokleides has danced away his bride,' to which the young man cheerfully replied, 'Hippokleides doesn't care!' This is why Athenians quip, 'it's all the same to Hippokleides' to indicate that they don't feel too strongly one way or the other about something.

The host should ensure that his guest is rested and well-fed before he settles down to satisfy his curiosity through a grilling about his occupation, his city, his family and his life and times. If host and guest get along well, the host will bestow a small gift on the guest's departure, thus signifying that they are now

Welcome, stranger. You shall be entertained as a guest among us. Afterwards, when you have tasted dinner, you shall tell us what you require.

HOMER • ODYSSEY • 118–24

xenoi, a pair bound by ties of hospitality which should be reciprocated when the host visits the guest's city. *Xenia* should not be undertaken lightly. It is a hereditary condition, and *xenoi* are expected to look after each other's interests, and even pay the ransom should the other be captured by pirates during the onward journey, or in war with the other's city. It was a wanton disregard for the sacred bonds of guest-friendship that put Paris so firmly in the wrong when he absconded with Helen, wife of his *xenos* king Menelaos, and so started the Trojan war.

When you captured Troy, you failed to kill your wife, though she was back in your power.
PELEUS TO MENELAOS ON THE RECOVERY OF
THE UNFAITHFUL HELEN FROM TROY IN
EURIPIDES • ANDROMACHE • 627

Since guests are generally male, they are usually received in an elaborately decorated room called the *andron* (literally 'men's room'). This room may have mosaics on the floor made of carefully laid naturally coloured pebbles, an early form of the tesserae of later ages. The *andron* probably opens into a narrow courtyard, where there will be a door to the street. There is usually an altar to 'Zeus of the courtyard' here, where religious family rituals are carried out. There may be a larger room with a porch, often facing south to catch the winter sunshine, which serves as the main living room. The house may have a second storey, and this is often used as accommodation for the slaves or for storage. Almost all windows look out onto the courtyard, so a narrow Athenian street consists of a corridor of blank walls and doorways. However, the antefixes – the capping tiles where the roof meets the walls – often sport floral decorations or small effigies of animals, real or mythological. Where windows on to the street exist, the rooms behind are generally workshops or retail outlets.

Keep wheat in the driest room, wine in the coolest room and art and fine furniture in the best-lit room.

XENOPHON
OECONOMICUS • 9

It is always an excellent idea for male visitors to make sure discreetly that they know which areas of this particular establishment are reserved for the ladies, and so avoid the dire consequences that may follow from inadvertently wandering therein. (Technically, of course, the entire house apart from the *andron* counts as the woman's domain, so refrain from going anywhere unless explicitly invited.)

A quick way to tell a host's status is to check the amount and different types of wood in the building. Attica is not well forested, but a well-off Athenian will like

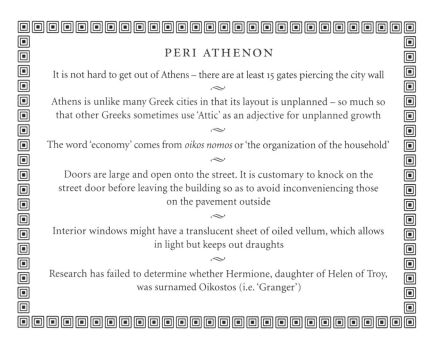

PERI ATHENON

It is not hard to get out of Athens – there are at least 15 gates piercing the city wall

෴

Athens is unlike many Greek cities in that its layout is unplanned – so much so that other Greeks sometimes use 'Attic' as an adjective for unplanned growth

෴

The word 'economy' comes from *oikos nomos* or 'the organization of the household'

෴

Doors are large and open onto the street. It is customary to knock on the street door before leaving the building so as to avoid inconveniencing those on the pavement outside

෴

Interior windows might have a translucent sheet of oiled vellum, which allows in light but keeps out draughts

෴

Research has failed to determine whether Hermione, daughter of Helen of Troy, was surnamed Oikostos (i.e. 'Granger')

cedar for staircases and doors, pine or fir for the floors, and oak for the window-sills and door steps. Roof-beams are often of cypress, and expensive furniture is inlaid with ebony.

ATHENIAN SOCIETY

People and Politics With the dust of the journey washed away, and wearing a clean woollen tunic (a *chiton*), the visitor is ready to face the extraordinary city of Athens. It has already been seen that Athens has some remarkable attitudes to women, foreigners and slaves, so it is worth taking a quick review of other aspects of Athenian society before plunging in. First, the Athenians are Ionians, a branch of the Greek people descended from King Ion. Ionians claim to be more intelligent and cosmopolitan than the stolid, humourless but dependable Dorians (of whom the Spartans are a prime example). Naturally, the Athenians claim to be foremost among the Ionians, if not the original ancestors of the clan, and this is one of the reasons why the Athenians feel a natural right to lead the Greeks of Asia Minor and the islands.

Although Athenians consider themselves unified with regard to ethnicity, when it comes to politics there are some deep rifts within Athenian society. Because of this some degree of caution is required when discussing politics –

There, with their long robes trailing, the Ionians gather, treading your sacred road, with their wives and children about them.

HOMERIC HYMN TO
APOLLO • 145FF

which the Athenians like to do all the time.

Political opinion in Athens is roughly divided into democratic and oligarchic. The oligarchs are those who fight for the privileges of the rich and aristocratic (or the greedy and oppressive), and the democrats fight for the common people (or a parasitic horde of layabouts). The relative opinions of each can be briefly summed up by the contrasting views of the democratic Perikles and a man known to posterity only through an anonymous pamphlet, who is generally referred to as 'The Old Oligarch'.

PERIKLES: *Power is not in the hands of a minority, but of the whole people.*

OLD OLIGARCH: *I do not approve of this type of constitution. For in choosing it the Athenians have decided that thieves should fare better than the best people of the state.*

PERIKLES: *No one is kept in political obscurity because of poverty.*

OLD OLIGARCH: *Anyone who wants, a thief maybe, gets up and makes a speech, and devises what is to the advantage of himself and those like him.*

PERIKLES: *We are free and tolerant in our private lives.*

OLD OLIGARCH: *The license allowed to slaves and foreigners at Athens is outrageous, you are not allowed to hit them, so the slaves don't even bother to make way!*

PERIKLES: We obey those in authority, and they obey the laws.

OLD OLIGARCH: They [the democrats] disenfranchise the elite, rob them, drive them into exile, or put them to death, while they exalt the thieves.

At this point insults start being thrown, followed on occasion by heavier objects, while the visitor discreetly retires from the fray.

However, with his claim that the 'best men' are driven into exile, the Old Oligarch has a point – Athens has a unique political institution called 'ostracism'.

Every year the Athenians get together and decide whether any member of the state is getting so full of himself that he is a threat to democracy, and they have a ballot on whom they think needs to be exiled from the city. On the appointed day they hand in their votes scratched on shards of pottery (*ostraka*), and the 'winner' of the reverse election is invited to take a ten-year holiday from the city. Thus, any Athenian who feels insulted or ill-treated by one of the Athenian elite can blow off steam by going home and smashing a pot (very good stress relief), gouging the name of the offending aristocrat into the clay and awaiting his day

'Old squill-head' Perikles likes to be portrayed with a helmet hiding his distinctive elongated skull.

[46]

Marked for exile. Ostraka *(pot shards) bearing the name of the 'potential tyrant' Themistokles.*

of vengeance. Once used, the clay fragments are very useful for filling potholes in the roads.

However, alarm that political discussions are about to break into open riot is seldom justified. The Athenians love a good argument, both in the sense of a shouting match and in the sense of a reasoned set of facts leading to a conclusion. And the more impromptu the better. It is a slight on an orator's character to suggest that he might have composed a speech while drinking water, rather than imbibing wine and pouring his feelings out straight from the heart. (Naturally, this impromptu speech should, as a matter of course, have perfect diction, an excellent argument and inspiring oratory. Athenians have high standards in this regard.)

> *We do not say that someone who stays out of politics minds his own business – we say he has no business here at all.*
>
> PERIKLES IN THUCYDIDES
> *HISTORY OF THE*
> *PELOPONNESIAN WAR* • 2.40

IV · ATHENIAN PASTIMES

The Academy § Cock-fights & Taverns
Shopping § Money

IN AN AGE EXPLODING WITH intellectual energy, Athens is the core which attracts new ideas, philosophies and inventions. This is one of the main reasons why so many metics abandon their native cities and come to Athens. New concepts might develop elsewhere in the Mediterranean basin but, like their inventors, they often end up in Athens to be debated and folded into the melange of ideas that make up the 5th-century intellectual revolution. The nature of infinity, the uses of steam power, the morality of eating beans and systems of astronomy are all meat and drink to the philosophers of the Agora. Although these men make up only a tiny minority of the Athenian elite, they represent the restless mental and physical energy of the city. If we are to describe Athens and its citizens in one word, it is 'busy'.

This energetic approach also applies to the Athenians' leisure time. They take this very seriously, and do not spend much of it relaxing. Leisure is as prized by the working classes as by the rich, and indeed, one of the main reasons for becoming rich is so as to enjoy more leisure.

Much of this leisure time is taken up with communal pleasures. The theatre has a recognized place in Athenian life, and it is well worth joining the large crowds that attend the annual competition (see p. 75) where playwrights display their latest offerings of comedy, satire and tragedy. Also, depending on eligibility, participation in the great religious festivals of the city is both interesting and a great social occasion.

This does not mean that Athenians do not make time for more unstructured leisure activity. As has been seen, Athenians enthusiastically enjoy discussion and debate, and just hanging around in the gymnasium or wine shop discussing politics, philosophy, war or sport is almost a career for some. (Visitors are welcome to join in these discussions as long as they remember their place.)

THE ACADEMY

AN ATHENIAN MALE WITH SOME free time might well take himself to the gymnasium, which is both a place of exercise and a social hub. Note that a gymnasium is not exactly a building, but a field and track where physical exertion takes place, although if the weather is bad, exercise might still be taken in a covered colonnade called a *xystos*. The Greeks include boxing and wrestling as athletic events, and anyone who wants to take part in the Olympics has to swear an oath that they have followed a serious training regime for at least the past ten months. (At athletic events married women are forbidden to watch the competitors – who generally wear nothing but a thin film of olive oil – but the spectacle is open to virgin girls.)

The Academy, with its famously shady groves protecting athletes from the force of the summer sun, is a good place to practise running and wrestling in warm weather. It lies outside the walls, northwest of the Dipylon gate, and is also where a number of philosophers and their students

Chaereas was walking home from the gymnasium; he was radiant as a star, the effort of exercise blooming on his bright countenance like silver on gold.

CHARITON • *CHAEREAS AND CALLIRHOE* • 22

pass their time. (A future student of Socrates known as Plato will set up a school here, which is why the name will be more associated with intellectual than physical activity in later ages.) The Academy is dedicated to its eponymous hero, Akademus, who is said to be buried there. (Akademus once helped with the rescue of Helen of Troy, and as Helen was from Sparta this place is particularly revered by Spartan visitors.) The Academy is also the starting place of a foot race which begins at the altar of Prometheus and finishes in the city. Because Prometheus stole fire from the gods, each of the runners carries a lit torch. Letting a torch go

Runners, wearing only a layer of olive oil.

out during the race leads to instant dis-
qualification.

Because Athens, like any 5th-century
Greek state, stands or falls by the
strength of its hoplite warriors, the gymnasiums are open for all to come and get
physically toned up.

*It was a sight to see the gymnasiums thronged
with warriors going through their exercises.*
XENOPHON • *AGESILAUS* • 50

When going to the gym, look out for
a man with a purple cloak and white
shoes. This is the *gymnasiarch*, the
elected official who runs the place, and
his staff is there to keep order. Staff, incidentally, does not mean personnel – it
means a large and solid length of wood
used for thumping miscreants. The *gymnasiarch* is usually wealthy, and runs the
gym purely for the prestige. He personally pays for the supply of olive oil
with which the athletes anoint and
clean themselves. (The Academy does
have a water supply piped in, but Athenians generally wash by rubbing themselves down with olive oil and scraping
it off with a curved metal instrument,
instead of relaxing in a bath with a
loofah.)

Wrestling matches are worth staying
to watch if one happens to be taking
place. Greek wrestlers possess a high
degree of skill – and need it, as wrestling
is a brutal business where sprains and
dislocations are common (although
head-butting is ruled out). However, this
is mild compared with the savagery of a

The pankration. *If you must do this sport,
it helps if you were ugly to start with.*

type of all-in boxing called the *pankration*, where boxers use leather straps in
place of gloves and aim principally for
the head and face. Intentionally killing
one's opponent in these fights is severely
punished, but an experienced boxer generally looks as though his opponents
have had a good try anyway. At the gymnasium most boxers wear padded head-
gear to save their teeth and cheekbones
from getting hammered in during com-
petitive bouts.

Both wrestlers and long-jumpers
make use of a sandpit, so the *gymnasiarch* has to decide who gets to use it
and when.

Field events include the javelin and
discus, and seeing these events being
done in full armour is another sobering
reminder that war is a very frequent
occurrence, and athletic practice at a

gymnasium is something between a leisure activity and a matter of life and death.

You'll go to the Academy, to race under the sacred olive trees, with a decent friend of your own age. Carefree, you'll wear your white reed garland, you'll smell yew trees, and the leaves which quiver in the poplars, while the plane trees whisper softly to the elms, delighting in the spring.

ARISTOPHANES • *THE CLOUDS* • 51

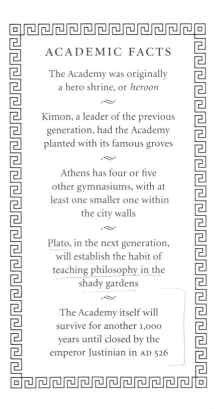

ACADEMIC FACTS

The Academy was originally a hero shrine, or *heroon*

∼

Kimon, a leader of the previous generation, had the Academy planted with its famous groves

∼

Athens has four or five other gymnasiums, with at least one smaller one within the city walls

∼

Plato, in the next generation, will establish the habit of teaching philosophy in the shady gardens

∼

The Academy itself will survive for another 1,000 years until closed by the emperor Justinian in AD 526

COCK-FIGHTS AND TAVERNS

BACK FROM THE ACADEMY, IN Athens itself, a noisy little crowd of shouting people probably means that a cock-fight is taking place. Athenians of all ages and social classes enjoy these events – the nearest Athens gets to gladiatorial combat – and they often gamble heavily on the outcome.

The gambling-place ... where the gaming-table is set, and cock-fighting and dice-throwing are the regular occupations.

AESCHINES • *AGAINST TIMARCHUS* • 53

The rich take this to extremes, and a prize pedigree fighting cock is worth a considerable sum of money. Because a fighting cock with his erect comb and strutting aggression is seen as a symbol of virility, it is a common gift which an older man might bestow on his *eromenos*, the teenage boy of his desire. Others emblazon a fighting cock on the shields of their hoplite panoply – a dangerous declaration, since the hoplite is signalling that, like a fighting cock, he is supposed to fight to the death. The violent masculinity of a fighting cock powerfully appeals to the macho Athenian male psyche, so fights are always well attended, whether impromptu affairs arranged by the poor on street corners or elegant prize fights in elite gambling clubs. However, the winning of his bout does not guarantee the safety of a bird. The testicles of a fighting cock are commonly believed to be a sovereign cure for

Two birds face off at the start of a cock-fight.

impotence – and the more victorious the bird, the more his virility is coveted. A champion prize-fighter might also end up immortalized in ceramic – vases featuring cock-fights are a common sight in the shops.

By night, the Athenians are emphatically party people. The rich like to indulge in symposiums. These are parties which may be refined affairs in which the protagonists drink watered wine and discuss the affairs of the universe (Socrates turns up at such affairs with unnerving frequency). Or, alternatively, they could be drunken orgies which end with the furniture being thrown around the room, black eyes administered in fights for the favours of flute girls and the entire party transferring to another house by wending its way through town in a drunken conga line.

The poorer people take their pleasures in the *kapeleion,* or tavern. The *kapeleion* is almost as familiar as a standard pub or diner. Dice and board games are available, but note that any females unwise enough to turn up on the premises are considered available too. The owner of the establishment will offer a selection of wine, and perhaps some fast food to go with it.

Those drinking late at night should make sure they leave with friends, and buy some torches to light the way home. Nocturnal violence is not uncommon in Athens, and muggers are particularly fond of snatching cloaks, which get a good price in the markets, for example that of nearby Thebes.

I was offered all sorts of good things in the taverns – wine-cakes, honey, dried figs

HERMES IN ARISTOPHANES
PLUTUS • 1120

Eiresione bring figs, and Eiresione
bring loaves;
Bring us honey in pints, and oil to rub
on our bodies,
And a strong flagon of wine, for all
to go mellow to bed.

PROCESSIONAL CHANT OF YOUNG MEN
IN PLUTARCH • *LIFE OF THESEUS* • 4

SHOPPING

REPLACEMENT CLOAKS, LIKE MUCH else, are to be found at the Agora, where you can choose anything between crude home-made cloaks of animal skins roughly sewn together to the finest Persian imports. The Agora is not the only market in Athens – there is another, for example, in a small enclosed building near the southern wall. But that is a minor affair with about a dozen shops and a small shrine, catering mainly to locals who can't be bothered to walk across town. The Agora is not merely a market (the name originally meant 'meeting place') and Athenians do not come only to shop, but also to meet friends and read the news. Public announcements are usually pinned up there, on a small shrine to the epony-mous heroes. (The eponymous heroes are those the ten tribes of Athens are named after.) Although a modest affair at present, there are plans afoot that will soon make this shrine into one of the major monuments of the Agora.

Shopping itself is remarkably basic. The Athenians are not great materialists,

and their homes are surprisingly, well, Spartan. What is available for sale at any given time may not correspond with the buyer's needs, for even in Athens, trading centre of the Aegean Sea, goods are not as readily available as they will be in later ages. This, combined with the laws of supply and demand, means that prices even of basic goods can vary wildly depending on the current shortage or surplus. As a rough guide, the standard Athenian ration of wheat is the *choinix*, a measure of about two pints, which is about enough to get a working man through the day. Depending on the time of year and the harvest, one drachma gets about 10–17 *choinikes* of wheat. Therefore, by picking those goods which are plentiful and cheap at any given time, a shrewd shopper can make five drachmas feed a family of three for a fortnight. Meat is not generally much in evidence, but stalls selling fruit and vegetables are well patronized,

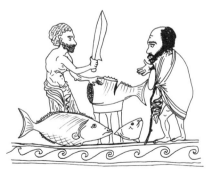

No one appreciates fish like the Athenians. You must bargain hard for the best cuts.

and you can get your lentils fresh or ready-stewed.

If determined to get meat, one might look for a stall where a hunter sells the hares that he has caught. Pheasants are available, but expensive. Alternatively one could visit a sausage seller's stand, but be aware that the contents of the sausage may not match the seller's glowing description. A better option might be fish. The Athenians have a passion for fried fish, and an *opsophagus* (fish-eating fanatic) will comment on an individual fish's texture and flavour as knowledgeably as any wine buff can talk vintages. He will

I scorn your red mullet and your eels.

PHILOKLEON IN
ARISTOPHANES
THE WASPS • 510

enthuse particularly about cuttlefish, and these command such high prices that Athenians regard the height of felicity as being 'rich enough to eat cuttlefish'. There is also a splendid selection of cheeses, with mainly sheep and goats' milk being used for local varieties.

Look out for elegant drinking horns. Curved and beautifully sculpted, often of Thracian metalwork, these generally have an animal head carved to form the base. A disadvantage of these horns (or advantage, depending on one's perspective) is that they are designed to be stuck into the earth between swigs. If you can't do this you have to lay them on their side – which involves drinking all the contents first.

Those of a practical bent might look instead for a *kothon*, or 'Spartan cup'. These are little jugs with deeply ribbed sides. The ribbing was originally used to trap sediment when water was scooped out of a river, but as the Athenians do not filter their wine, the ribbing works just as well to stop a drinker from imbibing the detritus that accompanies even an expensive vintage. On the other hand, those shopping for a taste of the esoteric might like to track down a dream-interpreter, who for two obols will explain exactly what point the supernatural powers are trying to make when they send that recurring codfish dream.

Lady shoppers, if they *must* be shameless enough to go to the market, should

Athenian men appreciate horses and wine – this drinking horn combines both worlds.

shelter their delicate features from Helios, lest the sun god inflict them with a tan – brazen is scandalous, but bronzed is outrageous. Therefore, look out in the first case for a *skiadeion*, a little folding sunshade. This can be carried by a slave or other male escort, whilst the lady shops for perfumes in little alabastrons – tiny pottery vases, finely made out of almost paper-thin material. There is also a variety of hairpins of metal or ivory with elegantly decorated heads. Earrings, pendants and bracelets abound, made of beads, bronze or semi-precious stone. Gold and silver are of course also available for the extravagant, but workmen tend to bring such prize artefacts directly to the houses of those who can afford them. Dresses are made of wool, *byssos* (a fabric so finely spun that it resembles cotton), or even Egyptian linen. Anything offered 'Amorgos-style' is definitely only for private use, as this is both very thin and revealingly transparent. Clothing is generally either off-white, brown-red, or, especially with women's *chitons*, a soft saffron yellow. Cloaks tend to be various shades of brown.

Shoes, as we have seen, are optional and if worn should be removed when going indoors. However, a generous selection are available for those who want them, ranging from the intertwined straps which make up the *sandalon,* to the knee-high *endromides* boot. Again, it may be a relief or disappointment to discover that high heels are not an option.

A cobbler at work making bespoke footwear to measure.

Markets are made more colourful by flower stalls offering narcissus, myrtles, roses and violets. Violets are so much a particular favourite of the Athenians that the playwright Aristophanes sneers 'when delegates from other cities wanted to deceive you, they just had to call you "the people crowned with violets," and at the word "violets" you immediately sat erect on the tips of your bottoms'. Flowers are often offered on the shrines of the gods, and those going to a party in the evening will be looking for garlands of blossoms to wear on their heads. The *stephanoi*, or flower-girls, have notoriously lax morals, and they might easily be persuaded to come along to the party along with the garlands they are selling.

Its cute that we us humans like to grow + collect Flowers just because we think they are pretty

MONEY

PRICES OF MANY GOODS AND services are regulated, but still expect to bargain for the best deals, starting with the money-changer who converts your cash. You probably won't get a one-to-one exchange for your drachmas, not least because Athenian money-changers understand that 'drachma' comes from the Greek verb *dratto* – 'to grasp'. Athenian drachmas (known as 'owls') are famously the hardest currency in the world. Thanks to the silver mines at Laurium, the drachma is full-weight pure silver. So respected is the unvarying format of its coins (Pallas Athena on one side, an owl on the other) that some states around the Black Sea have adopted the same format for their money. The ancient proverb 'bringing owls to Athens' has exactly the same meaning as 'taking coals to Newcastle' – you are importing what already exists in abundance at your destination.

That said, insist that your 'owls' are weighed before they are handed over. (There is an office at the Agora which contains a standard set of weights and measures, and market officials check that the scales used by traders conform with these.) It's a common trick to get a sheet of silver foil and wrap it around a hot copper base, then stamp a coin on that. The heat and the force of striking bonds the copper with the silver, and only the weight gives it away. Also make sure your coin is marked AOE, with the O having a little dot in the middle. That stands for A-T-H-E, and means that your coin is Athenian and not some low-value Black Sea knock-off.

One obol, placed over the eyes or under the tongue, accompanies the dead on their journey to the underworld as the fare for Charon, the ferryman who takes the deceased across the river Styx

～

The mother of the playwright Euripides is said to have run a fruit and vegetable stall in the Agora

～

One obol will get you a good loaf of bread, and maybe a cupful of wine to wash it down

～

An estimated 20 million drachmas were minted in Athens in the period just before the Peloponnesian war

～

A genuine drachma should weigh a little over 4.3 grams

～

The Athenian fondness for violets may date back to the time of the legendary king Ion (*ion* means 'violet')

CURRENCY

8 chalkoi	=	1 obol
6 obols	=	1 drachma
100 drachmas	=	1 mina
60 minas	=	1 talent

The largest denomination coin you are likely to come across is the tetradrachm, or silver stater, but it is not very common, as it represents about a week's wages for a skilled artisan. Even a regular citizen doing jury duty gets only half a drachma a day, so the regular currency of everyday commerce is chalkoi and obols.

Chalkoi are made of bronze, but the surprising thing about these everyday coins is how small they are. An obol is slightly less than 1 cm across and weighs less than a gram. A hemiobol (half an obol) is – unsurprisingly – half the size. This will delight later archaeologists as these tiny coins are constantly being lost down the back of ancient sofas, especially as Athenian clothing is sadly deficient in pockets.

In fact the usual place to stash enough money for a quick morning's shopping is in the mouth. A quick investigation with the tongue will reveal that the gum folds back against the front jaw to create a natural purse, and one which it requires considerable intimacy to pick.

A character in Aristophanes sums up these issues with money commenting 'Lysistratos played me a diabolical trick the other day. He received a drachma for the two of us and went to the fish-market to get it changed. Then he came back with three fish scales. I took them for obols and crammed them into my mouth.'

I had sold my grapes
and had my mouth stuffed
with pieces of copper – indeed
I was going to the market
to buy flour.

ARISTOPHANES
ECCLESIAZUSAE • 819FF

V · MEET THE ATHENIANS

Hyperbolos § Perikles § Socrates
Thucydides § Phidias § Aeschylus
Sophocles § Aristophanes

WHILE ATHENS IS NOT MUCH bigger than an average 21st-century market town, a truly incredible amount of brainpower is currently packed within its walls. The Athens of 431 BC can turn its nose up at Shakespearean London or Renaissance Florence – in terms of the number of geniuses Athens is incomparable.

Here are the men (and after what we have seen of chauvinist Athens, it should come as no surprise that they are men) who will change forever the way that Europe talks and thinks. If you consider this hyperbole let us visit **Hyperbolos** himself, a man who bequeathed his name to posterity through his speeches that deliberately exaggerate a situation to give it dramatic effect. He has proposed several sensible decrees, but his over-blown demagoguery alienates many – including Alkibiades, the man who will later contrive to have him ostracized. Thucydides, the master historian, is also evidently no admirer as his comment on the ostracism (above) shows.

The first genius one should visit practises in the field of politics, though 'practise' hardly describes the techniques of the master. This is the man the Athenians affectionately call 'old squill-head', **Perikles**, after whom this entire astounding era will be named.

Being a direct democracy, the Athenians do not have leaders as such – anyone can stand up in the assembly and propose what the city should do next. But the man whose proposals are most heeded is Perikles. 'He could generally keep the people with him, sometimes willingly through persuasion, and showing how best things could be done, sometimes very much against their will, forcing them to do what was good for them whether they liked it or not. He was like a skilful doctor coping with a complex disease – sometimes allowing the patient what would please him, while at other times administering drugs and pain that will work a cure.' Thus comments Plutarch, a biographer from later Roman times.

Perikles is a good, if cautious, general and a slightly unscrupulous politician. His exploitation of the unwilling financial contributions of Athenian allies is

> *[Hyperbolos]: a worthless character, ostracized not through fear of his power and reputation, but because he was a scumbag and a disgrace to the city.*
>
> THUCYDIDES · *HISTORY OF THE PELOPONNESIAN WAR* 8.74

directly responsible for the current economic boom in Athens.

It was Perikles who decided that those allied to Athens in the fight against the Persians should keep paying their contributions for the war, even though that war is now over. The money no longer needed for ships and soldiers should go towards restoring the temples in Greece destroyed by the Persians – starting (and finishing) with Athens. Since Athens is currently the only state in Greece with a huge and persuasive navy, her subjects ('allies' is the politically correct term) can do nothing but grumblingly pay their tribute, or, as Perikles would put it, their 'voluntary contribution'.

This has precipitated an epic construction programme that would take most cities many generations to bring to fulfilment. In consequence, smiths and carpenters, iron and bronze workers, stone-cutters, dyers, goldsmiths, ivory-workers, painters, embroiderers and potters are all hard at work, together with the suppliers of the raw materials. Merchants, sailors and ship owners all bring material by sea, cart-makers, cattle breeders, hauliers, rope-makers, flax-workers, shoe-makers and tanners all benefit from the boom times.

However, Perikles has his enemies, including one politician who commented: 'If I were to wrestle Perikles, and threw him fairly, he would win the bout by persuading the crowd, against the evidence of their own eyes, that the throw never happened.' Others do not trust Perikles because he is an aristocrat, and

very wealthy in his own right. He once had a magnificent building constructed by saying that if the state would not pay for it, he would do so from his own funds, and record the fact on the plinth.

However, if you want the real scandal about Perikles, seek out his son Xanthippos. Xanthippos has never forgiven Perikles for becoming estranged from his mother and taking up with the 'harlot' Aspasia. Xanthippos can generally be found in a tavern, beaker in hand, dishing the dirt on his father.

Perikles has an oddly elongated cranium (hence his nickname 'squill-head') which gives the comic poets plenty of ammunition. (One Teleklides describes him as 'fainting under the load of his own head'.) It is his sensitivity to such comments that has caused Perikles to generally wear a conveniently pushed-back helmet when his bust is immortalized for posterity – the shape of an Athenian hoplite helmet neatly conceals this embarrassing feature.

If Perikles is happily separated from his wife, then **Socrates**, the leading philosopher in Athens, is unhappily married to his.

Socrates is married to Xanthippe (literally 'yellow horse' – evidently a popular name for males and females) and has two sons. His fights with Xanthippe are legendary in Athens. After one such bout Socrates was drenched – some say with water, others allege with the contents of a chamber pot thrown by his furious wife. Socrates wiped himself off, commenting to his amused friends that 'after

Socrates, proof in stone that brains and beauty need not be found together.

the thunder, you can expect rain'. On another occasion when Socrates was at the market, Xanthippe ripped off his cloak. When asked why he did not return her blows, Socrates replied that Xanthippe was a wife, not a boxing partner.

This is not to say Socrates is a coward – quite the contrary. He is rich enough to afford a hoplite's armour, and has acquitted himself well in every action in which he has fought. The biographer Diogenes Laertius later recounted the story of one action in which, after the Athenians had withdrawn, Socrates followed the rest off the field like an offended cat, and turned savagely on any of the enemy who came too close. He also saved the life of the young Alkibiades

during a heated battle. Later, Socrates will display the same courage in politics, defying both the unjust orders of tyrants and the howling of the democratic mob. (It is, in fact, a democratic government which will falsely accuse him of corrupting youth and order him to commit suicide by drinking hemlock.)

A love of philosophy, as Socrates is the first to point out, does not preclude a love of the good life. He is more than happy to accept invitations to dinner parties or a good beaker of wine. Nevertheless, if these are not forthcoming, Socrates is prepared to be, well, philosophical about it.

Socrates is a sophist in his philosophy (*sophos* is wisdom and the origin of the word 'sophisticated'). As a sophist, he attempts to find the truth through following a line of argument to its conclusion. Along with his fellow sophists he is sometimes accused of teaching students how to make a weak argument sound stronger. Socrates himself denies that he is a teacher and doesn't take money for it, claiming that he simply discusses opinions with others. (The term 'Socratic dialogue' is named after his technique in which, by a series of questions, one person in a conversation forces the other to discover for himself the flaws in his beliefs.)

Socrates' deme is Alopece (southeast of the city wall), but the man himself is generally to be found in the Agora. Look for him, for example at the Stoa of Zeus Eleuthereos, where he likes to meet friends and pupils. He is easily

SOCRATES SAYS ...

TEN QUOTES FROM THE SELF-CONFESSED 'WISEST MAN ALIVE'

An unexamined life is not worth living

Wisdom begins in wonder

Get married or not – either way you will regret it

I am the wisest man alive, for I know one thing, and that thing is that
I know nothing

To live with honour in this world, actually be what you try to seem to be

If women were equal to men, they would be superior

If everyone's problems were put in one big pile for everyone to take equal shares,
most people would be happy to take their own and run

He is richest who is content with least. Contentment is nature's wealth

Every man should marry. A good wife will make him happy,
a bad wife will make him a philosopher

I was too honest to be a politician and live

recognized – simply look for the ugliest man on the premises. If you see a balding, scrawny individual with a pot belly, bulging eyes and thick, fleshy lips, you have probably found Socrates, the man that the Oracle at Delphi calls 'undoubtedly the wisest man alive'.

There are plenty ready to disagree with the Oracle, including the playwright Aristophanes who paid Socrates the compliment of making him the subject of an entire satirical play, *The Clouds*. Socrates (and philosophers in general) are shown as mocking the traditional gods of Athens, and teaching dishonest arguments. Aristophanes has a young man learning how to use Sophistic arguments to avoid paying his debts, and is taught by Socrates to disrespect his parents. The impressions

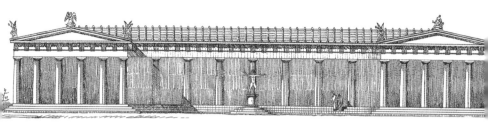

The Stoa of Zeus Eleuthereos, dedicated to the freedom Athens enjoys from Persian domination.

created by Aristophanes will contribute to Socrates' eventual condemnation and death.

They're a worthless bunch. I know them – you're talking about pale-faced charlatans, who haven't any shoes, like those rascals Socrates and Chaerephon.

PHEIDIPPIDES IN ARISTOPHANES
THE CLOUDS • 125

If interested in philosophers, it may be worth making your way over to the south of Athens, to the urban deme of Kollytos, and having a look at the house where, in two years' time, a muscular little baby called Plato will be born. He, the greatest of Socrates' students, will enlarge and develop his master's work as well as passing his philosophy on to later generations – Socrates, typically, does not bother committing anything to writing.

It is also well worth visiting another of Socrates' hang-outs, the Painted Stoa in the Agora. This was also where the philosopher Zeno used to teach, and indeed, this stoa is so associated with his

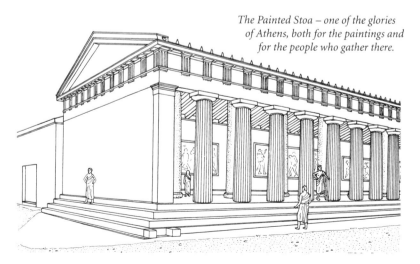

The Painted Stoa – one of the glories of Athens, both for the paintings and for the people who gather there.

teachings that even today we know his philosophy as Stoicism. The Painted Stoa is well worth a visit in any case, as it is one of the most famous buildings in Athens. It is also an excellent place to take in studies of philosophy. It is pleasantly cool in summer, and in winter its south-facing aspect ensures that the premises are gently warmed by the low-angled sun.

Those who prefer enquiries into the nature of things to be of a more practical variety should turn their steps to the rather aristocratic premises of Oloros, and ask for his son, **Thucydides**. Thucydides is a somewhat austere young man, given to sudden passions, yet his emotions are, with clinical deliberation, made subject to a cold, keen and dispassionate intelligence. His family is related to Cimon, a noted Athenian politician of the recent past, and the family have considerable influence in the gold-mining area of Thrace in northern Greece. When the war comes, Thucydides will unsuccessfully command troops in this area against the great Spartan general Brasidas. Thereafter he will turn his skills to chronicling the ebb and flow of the fortunes of Athens in its contest with Sparta and her allies. To do this, he will essentially have to invent the craft of writing history.

His famous predecessor in the field is Herodotus, a writer of the previous generation, whose *History* is a rag-bag of anecdotes, myths and travellers' tales. As a historian Herodotus meanders happily through this collection, getting sidetracked into endless digressions, yet always emerging triumphantly with the thread of his narrative. One imagines Herodotus as the sort of character who is surrounded by friends in a tavern, the wine flowing as he completes another of his yarns. One of the audience pours Herodotus another drink, and remarks, 'you know, you really should write a book about all this'. And so the *History* is born.

It is hard to imagine Thucydides in a tavern, simply because he does not seem to like people very much. His passion is for facts. He is practically alone among ancient historians in writing not to excuse or glorify the past, but simply to say what happened, and as far as possible to explain it.

With breathtaking self-assurance Thucydides says, 'I know some will find this history less interesting because it lacks the romance of myth. I will be content if my words are considered useful by those who want to clearly understand what happened in the past, since, human nature being what it is, this is going to happen again in much the same way at some time or another in the future. This work is not designed for the public of today, but to last forever.'

It is a testament to his skill that historians thousands of years hence will

The appearance of Sparta does not come up to expectations ... we have no right to judge cites by their appearance rather than by their actual power.

THUCYDIDES
HISTORY OF THE PELOPONNESIAN WAR • 1.10

talk of other ancient writers with either tolerance or exasperation, and with the understanding that their work is riddled with defects and foibles. Thucydides, however, will be talked of as if he is a senior colleague, who happens to have just left the premises. He is truly one of the greats.

Athens has a genius in almost every field, and those with a liking for the visual arts should head for the workshop of **Phidias**, though it's hardly necessary to go there to see his work – the spear and helmet of his massive bronze Athena Promachos on the Acropolis can be seen by those approaching by sea from from Sounion, 40 miles away. (*Pro-*

Zeus at Olympia, awesome in ivory and gold, one of the seven wonders of the world.

machos means 'who fights in the front line'.) Those who have come to Athens via Delphi will have also seen his work there, in a famous sculpture commemorating the battle of Marathon.

His masterpiece is unfortunately not here in Athens but at Olympia, where his giant statue of Zeus is regarded as one of the wonders of the world. To see this magnificent sculpture, the visitor walks into the chamber of the temple where the king of the gods sits enthroned in majesty. The statue is many times larger than the visitor, lifelike in ivory with a cloak of gold. (If rumour is to be credited, on his little finger is carved the name 'Pantarkes', who was the youth with whom Phidias was besotted at the time.)

However, it is not hard to see where Phidias found his inspiration. If passing the deme of Melite, close to Athens, look for a temple of Herakles which contains a very remarkable statue of the god. This is the work of Eleas, the teacher of Phidias.

Phidias has strongly influenced the design of the Parthenon, a creation which will be the iconic building of Athens ever after. However, it is unlikely that Phidias was personally involved in sculpting any of the Parthenon's famous friezes. They are marble, whereas his speciality is working in bronze, and no one does anything on the Acropolis who is not the master of his craft. Yet, as mentioned previously, his work can be seen outside the temple of the maiden goddess (*parthenos* means 'virgin') in his

Athena Promachos. The patron goddess of Athens is a ferocious warrior in her own right.

epic statue of Athena Promachos, and within is another of his masterpieces, an ivory and gold statue of Athena Parthenos herself. Athena is probably Phidias' favourite subject, but it is generally agreed that with Athena Parthenos the sculptor has outdone himself. Athena stands, golden and resplendent, protectress of her city. One hand rests lightly on a shield (on the decoration of which Phidias has introduced portraits of himself and Perikles), and the other holds out a statuette of the goddess of victory.

The reason why the statue of Athena Parthenos appears golden is that she is clad in gold – 44 talents of it, or 2,500 lbs. Thus Athena is not only the patron goddess of Athens, she is also the city treasury, and consequently access to the tem-

ple compound is not open to everybody. The gold of the statue has been designed and fitted in such a way that it can be removed should Athens ever have need of the bounty of the goddess. This, incidentally, is the reason why one can see everywhere the works of Phidias, his workshop and his students, but there is a distinct absence of Phidias himself – he has been exiled.

Due to his close relationship with Perikles in the works on the Acropolis, Phidias was an obvious target for the enemies of the present regime. He was accused of embezzling some of the gold now decorating his statue of the goddess, and when it became apparent that Perikles would be unable to protect him Phidias fled to Elis in southern Greece, there to execute the wondrous Zeus at Olympia described above. Not for the last time, genius was no protection from the petty politics and the jealousies of lesser men.

The students of Phidias still practise in Athens, but the deliberate archaisms of his style have given way to realistic, almost human statues. This is a somewhat disturbing development for some, since Athenian statues are painted and can look almost life-like. When, in a century's time, the great Praxiteles produces his Aphrodite of Knidos even that more sophisticated age will struggle to accept the concept of a sculpted female nude. This struggle can even become physical, and lithophilia – the act of attempting to have sex with a statue – will be a problem for a while.

Of course, any visit to Athens would not be complete without meeting at least one of the playwrights whose works will go on to grace the stages of theatres of the next few millennia. Sadly, one of the first and greatest of the original tragedians, **Aeschylus**, has passed on. Aeschylus fought the Persians at Marathon, and as well as being a leading light of the Athenian theatre, he travelled widely. He met his end in Gela in Sicily about 20 years ago under very unusual circumstances. An eagle had snatched up a tortoise, and looking for a rock to break the animal's hard shell upon, dropped the unfortunate creature with pinpoint accuracy on Aeschylus' bald head. Whether the tortoise survived is not recorded. Aeschylus did not. His sons keep alive his memory, and his plays are still often performed. Visitors who enjoy theatre should time their trip to Athens so as to arrive during the Lenaea or the Dionysia festivals, as many plays have their first showing at the competitions which are a major part of the celebrations. Also look out particularly for performances of Aeschylus' *The Trojan Women*, the gory *Agamemnon* or the epic *Seven Against Thebes*, as these plays are often shown during the Lenaea and Dionysia.

Perhaps the greatest living tragedian is **Sophocles**, who needs no introduction other than as the writer of *Oedipus the King* and *Oedipus at Kolonos*. The latter of these famous works was unfinished when Sophocles died, but he did manage to fit another 100 or so into his lifetime. Kolonos, incidentally, is the deme in which Sophocles was born. He was a handsome youth, which may be why he has a notorious sexual proclivity for pretty boys now that he is well past middle age (he was born in the 490s at the time of the Persian wars).

Like his famous predecessor Aeschylus, Sophocles is not merely a playwright – he is also a well-known man of affairs with considerable experience of warfare. On one occasion, when on a military expedition, Sophocles commented on the exceptional beauty of one of the

> *There's Sophocles, who is greater than Euripides.*
>
> HERAKLES IN
> ARISTOPHANES
> *THE FROGS* • 92

young recruits and was sharply informed by Perikles that a general needed not only clean hands but a clean mind as well.

Try not to disturb Sophocles at home. He is currently hard at work on his Theban plays, which will take all the awards in their class when presented to the Athenian public next year. Sophocles is not only the grand old man of Athenian drama, he is also pushing theatrical performances in new directions, expanding the role of actors and subordinating the chorus, which was once the main form of delivery in a Greek play. It helps that his doom-filled prose is limpid, clear and simple, yet poignant.

Yes, better hidden in Hades is a man plagued by foolishness, if he is from the lineage of the noblest of the enduring Achaeans. Yet he is true no more to the temperament of his forebears, but wanders outside himself. O Telamon, unhappy father, how heavy the curse upon your son!

SOPHOCLES • *AJAX* • 635FF

On the other hand, if high tragedy is not your cup of tea, and the struggle of man against gods and fate leaves you yearning for a good beaker of wine and some honey cakes, it may be the time to abandon the theatre for a few years until the works of **Aristophanes** hit the stage.

Where Sophocles is elegiac, Aristophanes is bawdy. While Thucydides writes his prose to be read forever more, Aristophanes stuffs his plays with in-jokes and references to contemporary affairs. His digs at those currently in power are sharp enough to practically skewer his victims. Indeed, part of the fun of attending an Aristophanes performance is to watch those being lampooned as they sit in the audience with fixed grins plastered grimly over their gritted teeth. Even the populace of Athens itself is affectionately teased, as in the following from *The Birds*.

Oh you, who have created your illustrious city in the air, you know not in what esteem men hold it and how many burn with desire to live here. Before your city was built, all men were fans of Sparta; long hair and fasting were in, men went dirty (like Socrates) and carried long sticks. Now it's all different. They are up with the dawn to get their food, then they fly off to peck at the notices and devour the decrees. The bird-brains are everywhere, so evidently many actually have the names of birds ... Menippus calls himself the swallow; Opontius the one-eyed crow; Philokles the lark; ... Midias the quail – actually he even resembles a quail that has been hit heavily over the head. People are coming here in their tens of thousands to ask you for feathers and hooked claws; so take care to lay in a supply of wings for the immigrants.

ARISTOPHANES • *THE BIRDS* • 1605 FF

At present Aristophanes is a young man, wandering wide-eyed about Athens, enjoying the boom-town feeling and the intellectual energy of his era, but already with an eye to the hypocrisy of those who exploit the allies they have made into subjects, and developing a contempt for the demagogues he feels are leading Athens astray. When war comes, he will be appalled by the senseless tragedy and waste of life, and his plays campaign intensely for peace. The first of his plays to survive for posterity – *The Acharnians* – describes a man who makes a private peace treaty to opt out of the war and benefits mightily in consequence.

For Aristophanes, the best of times is now. His later plays will often hark back to the present era when imperial Athens, unbruised by war or the ravages of plague, faces the future with sublime self-confidence. A typical Aristophanes character is something of a reactionary, disliking social change and wanting mostly to be left alone to enjoy life in the traditional style. This character is typically Athenian too, in that he (or she – Aristophanes is happy with female protagonists) is self-willed, tenacious and energetic, and quite prepared to use violence if it will help.

In terms of politics, art, theatre and philosophy the Athens of the 430s leads not just Greece, but the known world. The men described above are breaking new ground in their field, and laying the foundations upon which much of later western culture will be constructed. They are the second generation of pathfinders, building on the work of men like Solon and Kleisthenes in politics, and Aeschylus and Herodotus in the arts. Others will follow, whose names will be glorified by later ages – Plato, Aristotle and Demosthenes, to name but a few. Yet all will look back, and yearn to be in Athens as she is now, in the full glory of her golden age.

VI · ACTIVITIES

*A Morning at the Pnyx § An Afternoon at
the Theatre § An Evening Symposium*

DEMADES: *Demosthenes teach me [about
political rhetoric]? Athena might as well
take lessons from a sow!*

DEMOSTHENES: *That's the Athena who
was working the other day in a brothel
in Kollytus.*

PLUTARCH • *LIFE OF DEMOSTHENES* • 11

A MORNING AT THE PNYX

AT LEAST ONCE A MONTH (ALTHOUGH
not on days when the law courts are
sitting or during religious festivals), a
strange scene takes place in the Agora
and other popular spots in Athens.
Slaves appear, backed up by Skythian
archers. They draw red ropes across one
side of the market, and start walking
slowly forward. The women and slaves
present slip away, as do more than a few
of the men. The others go about their
business, but keep a wary eye on the
approaching line. While many allow the
rope to get close, everyone takes care not
to let it touch them. The dye in the ropes
is wet, and leaves a mark where it meets
clothes or flesh.

To avoid the ropes, the crowds drift,
slowly at first, then with increasing
urgency towards the Pnyx, about 400
yards to the southwest of the Agora. No
one wants to be last into the narrower

streets where the ropes can catch up as
the crush slows down the crowds. There
is a fine to be paid by the red-marked
laggards for dawdling on their way to
their duty of attending the *ekklesia* – a
meeting of the Athenian people.

The first thing to note about Athenian
democracy is that it is controversial. Not
just the political practice, which is bit-
terly resented by aristocrats up and
down Greece, but even the name itself.
Demos means 'the people of the masses',
and *kratos* means 'power' in the most
naked sense, so 'democracy' is actually
a rather negative term with connota-
tions of 'mob rule'. A more polite expression would be 'demarchy' or 'rule by the
people'. But many of the contemporary
writers on the topic are aristocrats, who
take the view that Athenian democracy
is akin to the principle of two wolves and
a sheep voting on what's for dinner.
They adjust their language accordingly
– and the usage will stick.

In fact, Athenian democracy is hardly
universal suffrage. It literally means 'one
man, one vote'. That's 'man' in the sense
of 'not female'. The title 'man' is very
specific – he cannot be underage (the
voting age is 20) or a foreigner or slave.
In fact, 'man' in the political sense is an
Athenian male citizen in good standing.
These criteria already trim the voting

base down to one in ten of the population in Athens, so the city is by no means empty during meetings on the Pnyx. As there are no proxy or postal votes citizens have to be there on the spot to make their opinions count. Some Athenians are away on business, war (the city recently took a pounding during a disastrous campaign in Egypt) or detained by family matters. So the 'pure' democracy of Athens might involve the votes of some five per cent of the population. Nevertheless, most Athenians are very proud of their system, so it is unwise to make the above comments too loudly.

In fact, if all 30,000 or so Athenians with voting rights turned up, there would be nowhere to put them all – which is why voting for ostracisms (which require a quorum of 6,000) takes place in the Agora. When several thousand assemblymen arrive at the Pnyx it gets uncomfortably crowded – indeed, the name 'Pnyx' has its root in the word for 'jam-packed'. However, for a routine meeting of say, 3,000 to 4,000 assemblymen, there is usually room for any non-voting spectators to have a look at the action, so feel free to stroll up the hill with the crowd, but keep a sharp eye out for the line of hurdles, policed by archers, which separates spectators from participants.

Physically the Pnyx is not much to look at – it is a south-facing hillside with a slope which allows people to look towards the *bema*, the flat-stone speakers' platform, at the base of the hill.

The nine officials who supervise the business of the assembly have some protection from the sun (rain, signalling divine displeasure, might bring events to a close), but everyone else sits in the open. And that, in terms of architectural splendour, is it. Yet this dusty slope is the site of the world's first regular democratic assembly, and as such is one of the most significant patches of land on the planet.

Once everyone has greeted friends, jostled for a suitable place and settled down, the assembly starts. Occasionally there will be cries of anger or denial, or even a small scuffle as someone is recognized who has no right to be there. An Athenian can lose his right to attend the assembly by owing a debt to the public treasury, assaulting his parents, having been struck off his deme's register of voters or ditching his shield so as to leave the battlefield in a hurry.

While everyone looks over his neighbours, and a general consensus forms that everyone present has a right to be there, various priestly types are purifying the area, while heralds call down ritual curses on trespassers and anyone who attempts to mislead the people. After this the actual proceedings begin with a standard announcement by the herald: 'Who wishes to speak?' In theory, anyone can get up and, if selected, sound off. However, it takes a strong nerve to give one's opinions to a crowd of thousands of highly critical listeners, and it takes equally strong lungs as well. Furthermore, most of the other speakers will be semi-professionals – the *rhetores*, or recognized orators. They will be more than happy to publically humiliate any amateur by delightedly dissecting any weaknesses in his logic or delivery. The vast majority prefer to remain average, non-speaking members of the assembly. These are generally referred to as *idiotes*, which is how many professional politicians have considered their voters ever since.

Generally, the matters to be discussed in the assembly have been prepared in advance by a committee called the *boule*. Embassies and ambassadors make their report directly to the assembly, and the assembly decides foreign policy according to what it hears. If the matter is technical, speakers are generally expected to have some expertise in their subject. But if the matter is political, anyone is welcome to have their say, be it a shoe-maker, a sea-captain or an aristocrat.

But if someone attempts to advise them on this [shipbuilding], and the people do not regard him as a craftsman, he might be rich, handsome and aristocratic, but that won't make them accept him. They will laugh at him, mock him and shout him down, until either he gives up and leaves in the face of the heckling, or the archers pull him from his place. If the presiding officials so decide, he can be kicked out from the assembly altogether.
PLATO • *PROTAGONES* • 319B–C

A man can commit no crime greater than telling lies to the assembly; for when politics is based on speeches, how can it be conducted if the speakers are liars?
DEMOSTHENES • *SPEECH ON THE EMBASSY* • 19.184

Kleon with his unseemly shouting and coarse abuse while on the speakers platform.
ARISTOTLE *POLITICS* • 28.3

Because the agenda is posted beforehand (look for announcements, for example in the sanctuary of Dionysos Eleuthereos, on the southern slope of the Acropolis) many will have arrived knowing how they intend to vote. Occasionally the *boule* has strong opinions on how they think the assembly should vote, and essentially look for ratification of their proposal (it is by no means certain they will get it). Obviously then, the *boule* has an important role in the Athenian democracy, so the Athenians limit the opportunities for politicians to get into it. Selection of the *boule's* members is random. Like jurors, the names of these and other important officials are almost literally pulled out of a hat, and in the course of the year no one can be sure what duties he might be called in for, but he can at least take comfort that each office can only be performed once by each person.

There are various types of assembly – some are for the purpose of passing decrees, which commit the Athenian people to a particular course of action. Others choose generals, or meet after a campaign to reward or censure current generals for their conduct. Other assemblies are to ratify or amend laws (laws are drawn up separately by another committee called the *nomothetes,* and published in advance in the Agora).

All this is supervised by the presiding officials, who have a relationship with the assembly similar to that of a lion-tamers and his animals. They are in charge until there is a general under-standing that they are not, after which events can turn very nasty. Through experience, the authorities have decreed a 50 drachma fine for physically laying into the officials, which protects their physical safety to some extent. Neverthe-less a wise official will generally know when to give way gracefully, although Socrates (naturally) will later single-handedly try to defy the assembly by refusing to allow the legalized lynching of some scapegoat Athenian admirals. (The assembly went ahead anyway and ordered the executions, then later regret-ted it, and passed laws against those 'who had led them astray'.)

It's assembly day, the morning is here, and there's no one at the Pnyx
They're chatting up and down the Agora, scurrying to dodge the vermillion-dyed cord ...
I'm here, thoroughly prepared to raise hell, wrangle and interrupt the speakers.

DIKAPOLIS IN ARISTOPHANES
ACHARNIANS • 19FF

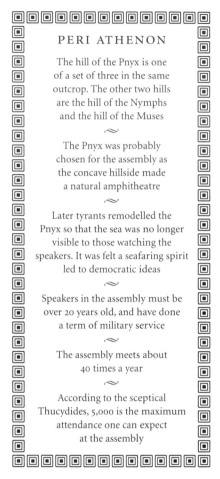

PERI ATHENON

The hill of the Pnyx is one of a set of three in the same outcrop. The other two hills are the hill of the Nymphs and the hill of the Muses

~

The Pnyx was probably chosen for the assembly as the concave hillside made a natural amphitheatre

~

Later tyrants remodelled the Pnyx so that the sea was no longer visible to those watching the speakers. It was felt a seafaring spirit led to democratic ideas

~

Speakers in the assembly must be over 20 years old, and have done a term of military service

~

The assembly meets about 40 times a year

~

According to the sceptical Thucydides, 5,000 is the maximum attendance one can expect at the assembly

Generally, proceedings are lively but controlled, principally because the Athe-nians expect a high standard from pub-lic speakers and appreciate it when a speech delivers this, which it generally does. When a demagogue gets up, for example the notorious Kleon, things get more high-spirited – to the extent where Kleon has occasionally to ask to be heard, at least until the basis of his proposal becomes clear. If the matter goes against him Kleon is quite up to shouting back and abusing his critics.

The presiding officials decide when the people have heard enough for them to come to a decision. The people will occasionally disagree, in which case discussion may continue. Eventually, however, the matter goes to a vote, which is basically a show of hands by those in favour. No detailed count is done, so if the matter seems close debate will continue or the matter will be postponed. In fact any business outstanding at dusk is deferred, because the vote-counting machines (the eyes of the officials with that job) do not work at night.

AN AFTERNOON AT THE THEATRE

COME TO ATHENS AT THE RIGHT time and a theatrical feast awaits. The right time is the 9th to 13th days of Elaphebolion (c. 24–28 March), the period between the first quarter and full moon of the month. This is the festival of Dionysos, timed for six months after the wine harvest, when the first vintages are ready for sampling. Athenians are never averse to an excuse for some drunken revelry, and the entire city likes to blow off steam during the festival of Dionysos Eleuthereos. Eleutherae is a deme on the borders of Attica with a special connection to the god. The

Maenads (female worshippers of Dionysos) play the double-flute and dance before his image.

[73]

legend goes that Eleutherae was independent, but opted to become a deme of Athens partly out of fear of nearby Thebes. As a symbol of unification, they sent an old but very revered wooden statue of their patron god Dionysos to the Athenians, who rejected it. Athens was smacked with a plague by the insulted deity and instituted the festival of Dionysos Eleuthereos by way of apology.

The festival begins with the 'bringing in' of Dionysos from his temple near the Academy, in a torchlight parade of young men who are gently drunk on wine. The sexual undercurrent often associated with the theatre is apparent in the goatskins on display (goats symbolize sexual potency) and the god's chariot which is pulled by a mule – being sterile, a mule indulges in sex just for recreational fun, and thus symbolizes pointless pleasure.

The next day an official procession comes to welcome the god, now reinstalled in his temple in the theatre district. Near the head of the procession comes the *kanephoros*, an aristocratic maiden who carries on her head a golden basket filled with offerings to the god. Grapes, the origin of Dionysos' favourite tipple, are prominent among these. Some of those in the procession wear crowns or garlands, others sport their best robes of purple, saffron and gold. Others wave huge phalluses to the accompaniment of bawdy shouts. This is a festival celebrating irrepressible life.

After the sacrifices, including that of the traditional blameless goat (the scapegoat) who atones for the sins of the many, the populace settles down to an orgy of some of the best drama that will ever be seen. Given that theatre as a genre is a single generation old, it is astounding that several of its greatest practitioners currently live in this single city, working on the plays which will be performed repeatedly for thousands of years.

A procession (with goat) approaches the altar.

Approach Maenads with care – once in their wild frenzy they tear animals apart and devour them raw.

So close to the Acropolis is the theatre that some of the hill has had to be carved away to allow the great open-air auditorium to sweep in a huge curved semi-circle about the stage and orchestra where the drama is focused. Behind is the *skena*, a solid two-storey edifice with pillars between, on which the back-drops to individual plays are either hung on painted canvas or set out on illustrated screens. The orchestra is the dancing ground where the chorus

There are other venues for theatre, and indeed some still imitate the original Thespians (see *peri Athenon*, right) and run their travelling theatres from the back of carts.

It is well worth visiting the Odeion of Perikles, a massive hall built into the south slope of the Acropolis. The roof is in the style of the Great Tent of the king of Persia, and slopes away on all sides from a single point. Since the Greeks captured the king's actual tent at the battle of Plataea in 479 BC, there is no reason to suppose this model is not reasonably accurate. The Odeion is used for musical events, especially involving song, and playing of the flute and *kithera* (a type of harp) during the Panathenaic festival. But for the full theatrical experience, there is only one venue, and this is situated right beside the Odeion. Here the competitors stage their entries for the play of the year, here the god blesses and encourages their efforts, here, in short, is the massive, imposing Greek theatre of dreams, the theatre of Dionysos.

PERI ATHENON

Sex and murder are unsuitable for public viewing and happen off stage (*ob skena*), so creating the later word 'obscene'

~

Tragedies may have started as funeral dirges for the blameless goats [scapegoats], sacrificed to purge the sins of the many

~

The acoustics of a theatre are mathematically planned before the building is started

~

Sometimes large earthenware urns are carefully placed in the auditorium to modulate the sound waves

~

Thespians take their name from Thespis of Icaria, the first actor known to have performed the lines of a written play in the 6th century BC

Comic actors sporting masks, padded clothes and dangling leather phalluses.

performs, and for a considerable part of the play it is the main focus of the action. Until recently it was the only focus, then the intellectual revolution of the 5th century saw the addition of actors to illustrate the deeds described in the *tragedoi* (goat-songs) of the chorus.

The morning plays are tragedies, plays with themes in which human nature and reality are brought into painful collision. They are skilfully crafted to produce an outpouring of suppressed emotion (*katharsis*) from the viewers, whilst the feeling of pity and sympathy evoked by a character (*pathos*) has given later ages the word 'pathetic'. Tragedy, along with

history, is among the most influential literary inventions of Greece, and it is here and now at this festival that tragedy as a genre is being given its definitive form. The plots are drawn from heroic and mythical themes that are well known to the audience through poetry, including the tales of Homer. Gods and gore are liberally interwoven into plots which feature sex, murder and random violence. The murder, like the sex, often takes place within the protagonist's family, but the actual killing happens offstage, and a variety of theatrical devices are involved in bringing the body onto the stage to be viewed in its heart-wrenching glory.

There is a strong musical element to these productions, with about five or so choral interludes per play, making Greek tragedy in many ways akin to opera. The entire complex performance generally is spoken in verse form (known as iambic triameter), something which many believe evolved from the other form of morning entertainment, the satyr play. Satyrs are semi-human creatures with an uninhibited lust for sex and wine. They are natural companions to Dionysos, and the plays that feature these mythical beings are one of the oldest forms of Greek theatre. The motifs of satyr plays deal with riddles, allegories of how fire, wine, music and so on came into the world, and how the satyrs accompanied Dionysos on his travels when Hera, queen of the gods, drove him mad.

Each play is introduced with a trumpet blast, and the audience have a good idea of what is coming as actors and playwright will have been introduced to the audience in a ceremony at the start of the festival. Much of the credit for a good play goes not to the writer or the actors, but to the *choregos*, the producer who put it all together. Because staging a play is an expensive business, doing so is seen as a *liturgy*, a service to the state, in much the same way as providing Athens with a warship or a public building is a service. The rich do this both to demonstrate their public-spiritedness and as a form of taxation. Sponsoring a play is a particularly worthwhile type of liturgy, because a winning play brings the sponsor enduring fame and political credit.

The bronze tripods which are awarded for the best plays are displayed along the road that leads from the sanctuary of Dionysos around the east and northeast sides of the Acropolis. They are inscribed with the names of the *choregos*, the musician, the playwright and the presiding Athenian magistrate.

Although some of the most memorable figures in Greek tragedy are women (for example Medea or Antigone), Athenian women do not appear on the public stage. Their parts are played by men, who easily carry off the imitation because the size of the theatre does not lend itself to subtle gestures or facial expressions. In fact facial expression is impossible, because the actors wear masks depicting the stock type of character they are playing. (If the play is a winner, the actors might afterwards dedicate their masks to Dionysos in thanks for his blessing.)

Having had their emotions wrung out by the dramatics of the morning, the audience retire for a fortifying lunch and a beaker or two of wine to prepare themselves for the afternoon's event, the comedy. At this time – and slightly later – there are five on offer during the festival, and the names to watch for are top playwrights Kratinus, Eupolis and (later) Aristophanes. It is strongly recommended that the delicate of disposition find themselves an alternative afternoon's diversion, as 'restraint' is only known to these writers in the context of physical bondage and sadomasochism. Uninhibited scatological jokes and

Comic actor. The large mouth on this character may have acted as a speaking trumpet.

this way is a reminder of the casual cruelty which is ever-present in Athenian life, even when the people of the city are at their most relaxed and jovial.

Whereas a tragedy usually has three speaking parts, comedy features four or sometimes more. Comic actors are un-encumbered by the heavy robes of the tragedian, and wear short tunics often padded to produce a grotesque effect. This is accentuated by the huge flapping leather phalluses worn between the legs of some actors. (The Greeks believe that smaller, perfectly proportioned genitalia are more aesthetically pleasing.) Gen-erally speaking, the comedy takes a real contemporary issue facing the city, and proposes a solution. The more outré and fantastical that solution the more it is appreciated by the audience. This results in a man mounting a flying dung-beetle to go to the heavens and personally peti-tion the gods about the state of the city, the embodiment of wealth (Ploutos) being brought to the city to chase out poverty and, on one outrageous occa-sion, the problems of Athens are solved by giving women the vote.

What gives the comedy its sting is that the abuse and vilification, not to men-tion the bizarre and burlesque, are simultaneously crude and highly sophis-ticated. The comedy borrows and sub-verts the traditions of the tragedies seen in the morning, and uses all the beauty and subtlety of the Attic tongue for its own disreputable ends. If the morning's tragedy is emotional *katharsis*, the after-noon is the political equivalent. In no

coarse sexual humour are combined with character assassination and polit-ical jibes in a pell-mell assault on the sensibilities of the audience, which gen-erally responds vociferously with com-ments, abuse and general pantomime-style heckling and booing.

Unlike the morning's genteel per-formances, females appear on stage. This depicts the nudity generally required by the plot more realistically. The roles are non-speaking, and the 'actresses' are slaves, both in real life and (generally) on stage. Their exhibition in

Archaic-style symposium guest. Longer hair tends to be an aristocratic affectation.

other time or culture do the leaders of a state permit themselves to be lampooned with quite the same degree of ferocity. To summarize – Athenian comedy is brutal, coarse, cruel, politically incorrect, and very funny. Go at your own risk.

AN EVENING SYMPOSIUM

I am about to entertain Autolykus and his father at a feast. I need not add that the splendour of the entertainment shall be much enhanced if my hall should have the good fortune to be graced by worthies such as yourselves.

XENOPHON • *SYMPOSIUM* • 1

A NYONE WHO KNOWS ANYONE IN Athenian society will almost certainly be invited to a symposium during their stay. Generally speaking, unless they are *hetaeras* (see below), or prepared to be known as such, ladies are

advised to decline such an invitation. Gentlemen ought to make careful enquiries before accepting an invite. A symposium may involve a discussion of Sophocles' use of divine allegory and whether the rhythm of beats in his triameters scan properly. Such a discussion might be accompanied by delicate lyre music and wine, diluted to the point of becoming grape-flavoured water. On the other hand, the symposium may be something considerably less refined, involving drunken carousing with naked flute girls, smashing of furniture and freestyle liquid eruptions all round. Or something between these two extremes. Select according to taste.

A further clue as to what the evening may bring will greet the visitor on entry. Some hosts use rose and myrtle fragrances for drinking parties, meadowsweet for when the mind should be kept clear. Gilliflower signals that delicate snacks may be on offer. The guests (usually 15 to 30 people) retire to the man's room, the *andron*, and settle on couches, one or two per couch. (Remember that the left elbow is used for propping oneself up, not the right.) The room is designed to point out discreetly that the host is a man of wealth and immaculate taste, so the couches will be decorated, as will the low tables beside the couches, and there will be expensive hangings on the walls. There is usually a decorative mosaic inlaid into the floor.

Remember that the key to a symposium is in the name – 'drinking together', so it is worth checking whether the invitation includes *deipnon*, a preliminary meal. If so, be sure to choose dishes well doused in olive oil to slow the entry of wine into the digestive system. Look, for instance, for *tagenitai*, wheat flour cakes fried in oil, although choose the version mixed with honey – the version with sea salt induces a thirst and undoes the careful preparation.

After the meal, the plates (and sometimes the tables) are removed and the symposium formally begins with prayers and libations. A libation is a liquid offering to the gods, in this case literally an invitation to the deities to have a tipple with the rest of the group. The symposium also formally finishes in this way, assuming that the participants are coherent enough to do so. The male participants are crowned with garlands purchased in the Agora that morning.

The key item in the room is the *krater*, a large wine-mixing bowl. Assess this carefully. Usually wine is mixed with water at a strength of three or four to one, making a beaker of wine about as strong as a glass of beer. There are small marks along the inside of the bowl, allowing the leader of the symposium (known as the *symposiarch*) to assess the group's progress towards drunkenness.

Among the group may be several *hetaeras*, a word which means simply 'companions'. As the 'as' ending indicates, these are females, but females who have at least one foot in the man's world of Athenian social life. Quite simply, these are ladies who do not play by the rules. They are not prostitutes (those are *porne* not *hetaeras*) yet they may be free with their favours, or have the attention of just one man. They are not courtesans, as they may be slave or free, and some may even be richer than any male in the room. Some are famously witty and sophisticated, and definitely no one's pet. The one thing they all have in common is they are not 'respectable'.

> *The Syracusans simply drink like frogs, without eating anything.*
>
> ARCHESTRATUS IN ATHENAEUS • 101C

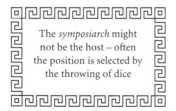

The *symposiarch* might not be the host – often the position is selected by the throwing of dice

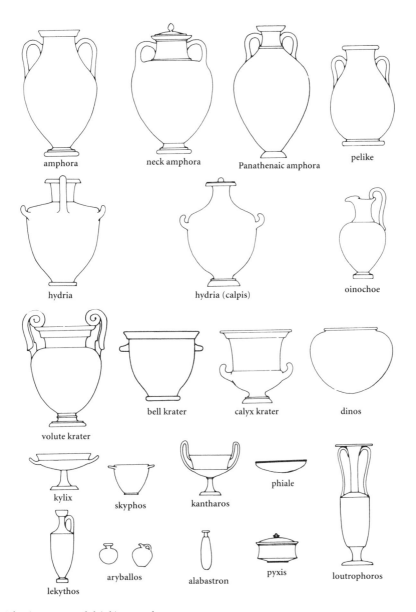

amphora

neck amphora

Panathenaic amphora

pelike

hydria

hydria (calpis)

oinochoe

volute krater

bell krater

calyx krater

dinos

kylix

skyphos

kantharos

phiale

loutrophoros

lekythos

aryballos

alabastron

pyxis

Athenian vases and drinking vessels.

These ladies drink alongside the men, and indeed may be the first to call on the host for larger cups to speed up the proceedings. The size of the cups on offer (these are a special type called the *kylix*) gives another clue as to what kind of proceedings the host as in mind. Small shallow cups (the type favoured by Socrates) suggest a thoughtful evening, perhaps discussing politics or analyzing social affairs. Large deep cups suggest perhaps a lively theatrical performance (in which the female protagonists are emphatically female) or dancing, or drinking games such as *kottabos*, in which the players attempt to toss the grape lees of their drink across the room to hit a saucer. The saucer is generally balanced on a candle-holder so that a successful shot results in it toppling off.

Hetaeras *are for pleasure, concubines for our day-to-day physical needs, and wives produce heirs and are sturdy guardians of the household.*

DEMOSTHENES
APOLLODORUS' SPEECH AGAINST NEAIRA • 59.122

Generally speaking, the evening starts in a genteel fashion, with the *symposiarch* introducing themes of conversation for the group to discuss. At this point it is unmannerly to have private discussions with those around you, as this is contrary to the general idea of group bonding which is what the symposium is for. Comments should be addressed to the room as a whole, and it is a matter of courtesy (and fine social judgment) not to say either too much or too little.

As the evening progresses the event becomes less formal. It now becomes permissible to have discussions in smaller groups, and some settle down to play board games, dice or *kottabos*. However, not all symposiums go even this far. Some of the more refined symposiums start and end with wine and conversation.

WINE KRATER REFILLS (IN DIONYSIAN MEASURES)

One krater • (by itself miserly) brings health

Two kraters • (the acceptable minimum) love and pleasure

Three kraters • (standard) sleep

Four kraters • (steady now!) hubris – overweening pride

Five kraters • (losing it) general uproar

Six kraters • (lost it) drunken debauchery

Seven kraters • (well out of hand) fighting and black eyes

Eight kraters • (chaos) the neighbours call the authorities

Nine kraters • (alcohol poisoning sets in) vomiting

Ten kraters • (it will take months to live this down) madness and throwing of furniture

After the libation and chant to the god and the other customary acts, they started drinking. Then Pausanias remarked: 'Well, gentlemen, what style of drinking should we have? To be honest, I am in very poor shape after yesterday's session, and I need a break.'

PLATO • *SYMPOSIUM* • 176A

To promote the revelry at this point, professional entertainers may be brought in. For example, there might be a flute girl, and next a dancing girl, skilled in all kinds of acrobatics, and a beautiful boy, whose graceful harp playing and dancing delight the guests. Often these entertainers are an organized troupe who make their living from appearing at such functions. In Xenophon's *Symposium*, the proceedings finish with a small play between a boy and a dancing girl showing the romance of Dionysos and Ariadne. The acting is so erotically charged that afterwards a substantial proportion of the gathering take themselves speedily homeward to the pleasures of the marriage bed.

You have not observed that a man would find it hard to insert a hair into any break in your talking, let alone a single grain of sense

HERMOGENES TO SOCRATES IN XENOPHON *SYMPOSIUM* • 6

At less refined affairs, participants don't bother heading for home, and the gathering breaks down into an orgy, with uninhibited couplings or group sex between guests and entertainers on the couches. At this type of symposium and at this stage in the evening, the male-female imbalance is generally evened out by those male protagonists laid low by Dionysos, and snoring quietly under the table with no further interest in proceedings. If, on the other hand, the symposium appears to be dragging to a quiet close, some of its livelier members may form a kind of conga line (*komos*) and dance their way through the streets to another party. Since these groups have a high proportion of testosterone-charged young men, they are best avoided as they make their merry way along. When two such groups collide in mid-street, as happens on occasion, nearby householders are treated to an all-in wrestling and boxing melee which lasts until the City Watch break it up with large sticks.

VII · A CITY OF GODS

*Hephaestos & Friends § Athena
& the Panathenaia § The Eleusinian
Mysteries § Witchcraft & Superstition*

ATHENS CONTAINS SOME OF THE first people in the world to start thinking about the universe as a machine. These people are philosophers, 'lovers of wisdom', and they look for a natural cause of things rather than simply attributing any inexplicable phenomenon to 'the gods'. Thus Thucydides, considering tsunamis, reflects that these generally occur in conjunction with earthquakes, and decides that the tsunami must be caused by a massive movement of the seabed, 'otherwise I do not see how such a thing may happen'. This is a revolutionary, not to say heretical, statement. Previous generations would have stated firmly that the tsunami happened because Poseidon, god of earthquakes and the sea, willed that it should happen, and that was that.

Nevertheless, it is a mistake to assume that Athens is a city ruled by empirical rationalism. In the city the gods are everywhere – Athenians firmly believe in them, and open atheism can be dangerous, if not fatal. The Athenians do not associate atheism with rationality. To

> *Once people could not tolerate philosophers, believing them to lessen the divine powers by making them simply blind forces operating through the laws of nature and necessity, rather than as free agents.*
>
> PLUTARCH
> *LIFE OF NIKIAS* · 23

them, not believing in the gods is like not believing in the Agora, or alleging that Spartans don't exist. Of course there are gods, although their exact nature is open to discussion. But Athenian gods are like Athenians in general. They don't like to be slighted or ignored, and are somewhat indiscriminate in their retaliation. The reason the Athenians don't like atheists is that they might be living next door to one when the gods decide to act on it.

HEPHAESTOS AND FRIENDS

ONE DOES NOT LOVE THE GODS (except in the case of Zeus, who believes in love in the carnal sense and is ready to indulge in it abundantly with the female half of humanity). Nor does one worship the divine perfection of the average Athenian deity. The gods of Greece are far from perfect, and nowhere near omnipotent. They possess all of humanity's faults and have a few more unique to themselves. One should think of them as embodying the forces which make the world work.

Demeter, goddess of the field, breathes life into the kernel of grain in the moist warmth of the earth, and sees an empty field grow into waving golden abundance. Artemis, virgin goddess of the hunt, pumps excitement into the veins of hunter and prey. At her will the questing pack finds or loses the scent, or the arrow misses or hits its mark. Ares, stern god of war, inspires or blinds the generals, fires up or demoralizes the armies, and determines, when the armoured hoplites meet shield to shield, which side will gain the victory. To deny these gods is to deny that the corn grows in the fields, to deny that winter turns to spring, to claim that inspiration never visits the poets, and to claim that when a man goes to war, to the hunt or to the sea, his fate lies entirely in his own hands.

Ares is a democrat –
there are no privileged
people on a battlefield.
ARCHILOCHUS • FRAG 3

Let us consider Hephaestos, god of craftsmen and the forge. An Athenian hoplite going into battle (and most Athenian males will go into battle several times in their lives) may or may not worship Hephaestos. But you can bet that this warrior sincerely hopes that the craftsman who made his helmet, shield and spear does so punctiliously. (This is particularly important as the Greeks of this period have not fully mastered the art of adding carbon to iron to make steel, so the quality of any given product can vary alarmingly.)

Hephaestos is a very 'human' god. He is small and has crippled feet, and because of this his mother, Hera, tries to pretend he does not exist. But Hephaestos is wilful, crafty and vindictive (he can't hold his drink either, but that's another story). He forced the other gods to give him Aphrodite as his wife. When Aphrodite betrayed him by taking the handsome Ares as a lover, he trapped the pair in a golden bed and brought the other gods to mock their shame. Hephaestos has a particular significance to

Women prepare oxen for sacrifice.

*Hephaestos at work, here preparing
the armour of Achilles.*

the women of Athens, for not only is he the brother of Athena, but he is the creator of Pandora, the woman from whom they all are descended.

Hephaestos has his own temple, the Hephaisteion, in the heart of the metal-working district on the hill west of the Agora. This temple is a perfect example of the severely practical Doric style, and is well worth a visit, not least for the wonderful friezes depicting the labours of that all-Athenian hero, Theseus. The temple is surrounded by a *peristyle*, with six columns across the front and 13 down the sides. The temple is the home of the god, and despite its appearance the design is quite homely; there is a front porch (the *pronaos*), a back porch (the *opisthodomos*) and a *cella*, which makes up the indoor section. Hephaestos shares his temple with his sister, in her aspect as Athena Hephaistia, and statues of the pair occupy a room within. After paying their respects to the powers symbolized by these statues, visitors might also want to take the time to admire the craftsmanship of that splendid bas relief of Theseus and the Minotaur.

The Hephaisteion is particularly worth visiting in the summer, when those looking for a break from the noise, dirt and heat of the metal-working district come to enjoy the flowers in the sanctuary's shady, well-watered gardens,

---

TEMPLE GEOGRAPHY FOR BEGINNERS

Sekos · main room of a temple, where the god is housed

Cella · the indoor section of a temple

Pronaos · the entrance hall/portico/porch (depending on architectural taste)

Opisthodomos · a sort of *pronaos* at the back (optional, and often not included)

Antae · extensions of the side walls to form a small portico

Prostyle · where the portico is formed by pillars instead of walls

Amphiprostyle · with front and back portico

Pteron · the space between the wall and the *peristyle*

Peristyle · a row of outer pillars around the temple

Stylobate · the top of the foundation which raises the temple above ground level

---

[86]

or to lounge in the deep shade of the *prostyle* portico.

ATHENA AND THE PANATHENAIA

AND WHAT OF ATHENA HERSELF, the virgin, grey-eyed goddess, who looks down from the Acropolis over the city where she is patroness and protector? She owes her birth to her brother Hephaestos, for when her mother, Metis (the personification of rational thought), was pregnant, Zeus swallowed her whole. However, Hephaestos seized an axe and split open Zeus' forehead, and Athena emerged, complete with the armour in which she is generally clad. In fact, there are several tales of the birth of Athena, including one in which her father was not Zeus at all but the winged giant Pallas. Athena later hunted Pallas down and killed him for trying to violate her chastity (the Greek gods have never got to grips with the ethics of incest). It is from him that Athena gets her name of Pallas Athena, and her alleged father's skin now provides the cover for her legendary shield.

Pallas Athena, most honoured goddess with all-seeing grey eyes.

Wise one, relentless in purpose, modest Virgin, protectress of the city!

HOMERIC HYMN • 28

In Athena, power and intellect are harmoniously combined. She showed the city's people how to yoke oxen and use numbers. She taught them the use of the trumpet, the chariot and the arts of navigation. From her comes the invention of money, and this is partly why Athena's owl, symbol of her city, is to be found on every silver drachma.

The Parthenon, 'the maiden's temple', is perhaps the most beautiful building to be found in the world. It is both a home to Athena and a perfectly proportioned sculpture in stone. The third day of every month is sacred to Athena, but to really see goddess and people as one, the best time to be in Athens is for the Panathenaia, and particularly for the Great Panathenaia, though the latter, like the Olympics, happens once every four years. Like the Olympics the Panathenaia features games, together with theatrical and sporting events, but the competition is limited to the peoples and demes of Attica, and second and third prizes are given as well as a crown to the victor. The entire festival is a huge family celebration of the Athenian people.

The festival begins on the 28th day of the month of Hekatombaion. (This is about mid-July to mid-August, although Athenian months and dates tend to be flexible affairs. The authorities are quite capable, for example, of adding a few extra days to a particularly busy month.) The festival starts with the ritual lighting of the sacred fire in the temple of Athena Polias, on the Acropolis just north of the Parthenon. (We see again that connection between Hephaestos and his sister.)

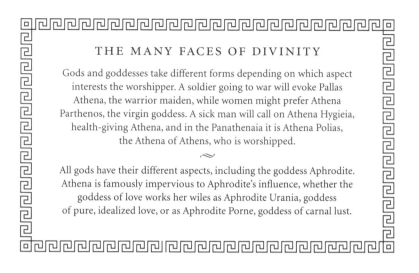

THE MANY FACES OF DIVINITY

Gods and goddesses take different forms depending on which aspect interests the worshipper. A soldier going to war will evoke Pallas Athena, the warrior maiden, while women might prefer Athena Parthenos, the virgin goddess. A sick man will call on Athena Hygieia, health-giving Athena, and in the Panathenaia it is Athena Polias, the Athena of Athens, who is worshipped.

~

All gods have their different aspects, including the goddess Aphrodite. Athena is famously impervious to Aphrodite's influence, whether the goddess of love works her wiles as Aphrodite Urania, goddess of pure, idealized love, or as Aphrodite Porne, goddess of carnal lust.

The second day starts with a large procession which forms at the Dipylon gate. Old men solemnly carry olive branches, young girls carry sacrificial cups and bowls while others bear sacred baskets filled with sacrifices to be dedicated to the goddess.

The procession is to bring Athens her new robe, her *peplos*, which is changed every year. Weaving this robe is the task of the young women of Athens, under the guidance of the *arrephoroi*, the virginal attendants of Athena. The weaving begins nine months previously at the festival of Athena Ergane. The robe is then ritually washed at the festival of Plynteria, and now forms the centrepiece of the procession, where it is mounted like the sail of the olive-wood 'boat' which moves with the chanting throng. From the Dipylon gate the crowd is led by the *kanephoros*, a young maiden selected from the aristocratic girls of Athens for her intelligence and purity. These qualities in the girl please the goddess – which is important, as it is through the *kanephoros* that the Athenians offer to their protectress the first fruits of the harvest of Attica.

The solemn yet joyful crowd move through the Agora and pause to sacrifice on the hill of the Areopagus (where murder trials take place at the end of each month). Thanks are given to the goddess at the temple of Athena the Victorious for guiding the wisdom of the generals, and for leading Athens to success in war. The huge gateway of the Propylaea is still under construction, and here many of those in the procession peel off to continue the festivities in their own homes or with friends. Only true-born Athenian citizens are permitted to continue to the great altar of Athena at the Erechtheion, on the north side of the Acropolis. There sacrifice is

VII *The Olympian gods battle the giants in the eternal struggle of intellect and order against unreason and chaos. Athena (centre) fights in her all-protecting aegis, whilst Hera, queen of the gods, makes herself useful with a spear. Beside her, Zeus prepares to hurl another thunderbolt into the fray.*

VIII (Previous page left) *Dionysos, clasping a kantharos (a heroically sized wine cup) receives an offering of a hare and a small deer from two of his maenads. The female followers of the god have pale skins in contrast to Dionysos' dark features, and each of them is holding a stylized sprig of ivy.*

IX (Previous page right) *Theseus and Poseidon clasp hands. Poseidon, failed candidate for the patronage of Athens, has a footrest decorated with tiny dolphins, whilst Theseus is standing and simply dressed. A krater such as this fetches a good price in the market as it is by a well-known artist (the Syriskos painter).*

X *The olive, the most welcome of the gifts of Athena to her people. Here, at the harvest, a climber bends the boughs so that the olives can be beaten off by men with long flexible sticks, while a fourth worker collects the fallen fruit.*

XI (Right) *Athena watches with interest as the intrepid Jason is disgorged by a dragon. Athena has her usual equipment of helmet and spear, although she carries an owl in place of her shield. However, she wears the aegis, a shawl with the gorgon's head that protects her from all harm, so the shield is redundant in any case.*

XII *If you are going to drink heroically, you should buy a cup to match. Here Herakles stares from the base of a wine cup, his head fringed with the fangs of the lionskin he wears over his head and knotted around his neck. The skin came from the dreaded Nemean lion which Herakles slew as one of his 12 labours.*

XIII (Right) *Satyr players assume their costumes, with one actor contemplating his mask while another, playing Herakles, is already fully attired with lionskin and club.*

XIV *Mother and son. Athena leans forward to accept the baby Erechthonios from Gaia, the Earth. The child was conceived from the earth (chthonos) after Athena discarded a semen-stained piece of wool there, following a failed seduction by Hephaestos. Erechthonios became king and honorary ancestor to all Athenian men.*

made, not to Phidias' towering sculpture of Athena, but to the wooden effigy of the goddess which in legend was given to the Athenians by the gods. Beside this stands an olive tree, the most welcome of the many gifts Athena has given to her people.

THE ELEUSINIAN MYSTERIES

ANYONE ASKING AN INITIATE what exactly happens at the Eleusinian Mysteries will be informed that telling the secret must be followed by killing the listener. This merry quip becomes less merry with the discovery that in fact the initiate is totally sincere – he must either do that or risk facing the

PERI ATHENON

Athena's robe is embroidered with scenes of the battle between gods and giants in which she played a leading part

~

In battle Athena wears the terrifying aegis, a shawl fringed with snakes' heads which is impervious even to the thunderbolts of Zeus

~

No other Greek god or goddess has a major city bearing their name

~

Athena is always shown with a helmet which is pushed back to reveal her face

executioner himself. For further details look at the death warrant for Diagoras of Melos, applicable anywhere in the Athenian empire, on the charge of discussing the Mysteries too freely.

The Eleusinian Mysteries are taken seriously because they honour the goddess Demeter, and when the goddess of all that grows in the earth is annoyed, the rains do not fall and the crops fail. The world has had experience of this before, when Zeus colluded with Hades, the god of the underworld, to kidnap Demeter's daughter Persephone. Outraged by her loss, Demeter went on strike, angering the gods as no wine or animals were available for sacrifice to them. The innocent party, the human race, of course suffered doubly.

Demeter not only withdrew her labour from Olympus, the home of the gods, she also withdrew herself, and settled at Eleusis in Attica, where a temple was built in her honour. Eventually a deal was worked out between Demeter and the offending gods, and Persephone was returned to her mother. The earth bloomed once more, but in accordance with the deal Persephone returns every year to Hades for four months, and during these months Demeter sulks, no rain falls and the earth slowly dries up. Some believe that Eleusis is where Persephone returns to her mother after her underworld sojourn, and the initiates of the Mysteries actually see the annual reunion of Demeter with her daughter. I could tell you if this is true, but then ...

Demeter (left) and daughter Persephone honour Triptolemus, the inventor of the plough.

Perhaps the best way to find out is by becoming an initiate in the Mysteries. The qualifications are not demanding. Initiates must not be barbarians (i.e. they must speak Greek) and they must not be polluted by blood-guilt (guilt from a killing must have been atoned for and the perpetrator ritually purified). Also, one requires a sponsor from one of the leading families of Eleusis. Apart from that, anyone, man or woman, Athenian or foreigner, slave or free can become an initiate. The only other criterion is not to speak about what has been seen – and in the course of two millennia, tens of thousands will behold the sacred ceremonies, and all will keep this promise.

Athens has produced many excellent and indeed god-like institutions. All of these have enriched the human experience, but I don't

PERI ATHENON

Diagoras, an infamous atheist, once chopped a wooden statue of Herakles into firewood, commenting that the demi-god's 13th labour would be to boil his turnips

~

Aristophanes, Plutarch, Sophocles and Pausanias are among those who are or will be initiated into the mysteries

~

The procession from Athens to Eleusis covers 13 miles, a pleasant stroll by Athenian standards

~

As well as being a sacred site, Eleusis is one of the main military bastions guarding western Attica

Persephone is also known as Kore, goddess of youth and joy, but as the wife of Hades she is queen of the dead

~

Demeter and Persephone are often depicted with corn, a sceptre and poppies

~

As befits a goddess of the corn, Demeter has shining blonde hair

~

The road to Eleusis is called the Sacred Way and is lined with shrines, graves and votive offerings

think any is better than the Mysteries ... They teach us the origins of life, and enable us not only to live joyfully, but also to feel hope in death.

CICERO • *THE LAWS* • 2.14

The end of the hot, dry summer is an occasion for general celebration, and it is welcomed by parties and ceremonies in Athens itself. But those preparing for initiation to the Mysteries will await the formal celebration, which happens over nine days in the month of Boedromion (late September).

On the day before the celebration begins, a large crowd of participants gathers in the deme centre of Eleusis. From there one of the ritual parades of which the Athenians are so fond winds its way with much pomp and ceremony back to Athens and the sanctuary of Demeter in the Agora.

The festival begins here the next day (15 Boedromion) with an announcement calling for initiates to take part. Each prospective initiate, a *mystes*, will have been given some training and guidance by a sponsor, a *mystagogos* – someone who has already been through the experience. Some who present themselves to the summons will be *mystes* returning a second time for further induction into the deepest secrets of Eleusis. Such people are known afterwards as *epoptes*.

The ritual continues for the initiates with a journey to the bay of Phaleron, there to wash and purify the body. Each initiate carries with them a piglet for sacrifice to the gods of the underworld. (Pigs are very acceptable to the gods, for they are highly fertile and able to find roots and buried tubers. The blood of sacrificial pigs mixed with seed grain leads to abundant crops.) As the initiates sacrifice, so too does the general population in public ceremonies and sacrifices to Demeter in Athens.

On the fifth day of the ceremony the celebrants return to Eleusis, bearing with them the statue of Iacchos, the boy demi-god who is a favourite of Demeter. Those in the procession cheer, and call out Iacchos' name, and regard with awe the sacred *hiera*, container of the symbols of the inner Mysteries, as this accompanies the procession.

Arrival in Eleusis is followed by a time of contemplation and fasting, broken by a drink of mixed grain meal and water, the same drink, according to the Homeric hymn to Demeter, that the goddess drank while awaiting the return of her daughter. For those who have never seen it, this is also a chance to visit and admire the Telesterion at Eleusis, the Hall of the Mysteries, which holds the cult statue of Demeter. This massive building has no windows, and a forest of internal columns, while the outside is magnificently decorated with friezes and statuettes.

Once prepared, the initiates go inside the inner sanctum of the goddess, and vanish behind the veil of secrecy which shrouds this awe-inspiring event. We are told that the high priest and priestess of Demeter reveal the contents of the *hiera*, objects passed to mankind in person by Demeter and Persephone, but what else happens is unknown, as is the nature of the sacred objects which are displayed. Almost certainly they deal with the return of life from the dark, of death and rebirth, and reunion with loved ones – but those who know do not tell.

Afterwards there is feasting and the sacrifice of a bull and dancing in the nearby fields, but the initiates in the Mysteries are notably less inclined to merriment. They pour a ritual libation to the gods, and at the end of the festival there is no final ceremony. After the Mysteries, this would be an anti-climax. Instead, the initiates return home, alone or in groups, reflecting on what they have experienced.

But when the earth starts blossoming with a new season, full of fragrant flowers, flowers of every sort, then is the time you [Persephone] must come up once more from the misty realms of darkness, to the wonder of gods and mortal humans.

HOMERIC HYMN • 400FF

WITCHCRAFT AND SUPERSTITION

Athens has shrines, temples and sanctuaries aplenty. Religious symbolism can be seen outside every house and at every street corner, yet surprisingly, a character who remains well in the background is the priest. Athenians, being Athenians, like to deal with their gods directly. They would not think of going to a priest for family advice or pastoral care. For them, a priest is a religious technician, a man who can instruct on the proper forms of sacrifice, and tell you the appropriate time of the month for rituals. Those wanting special favours from the gods, or from lesser powers and spirits, need to consult a witch.

Witchcraft is not strictly illegal, but it is pretty disreputable nevertheless. For a start, it is generally the province of barbarians – Skythian sorcerers and the like, and secondly, the major practitioners are not only barbarians but women. The archetypal witch is Medea, a woman of fearsome power who protected Jason and his Argonauts with potions and charms, and who slowed the pursuing Colchian ships by cutting her own baby brother to pieces and throwing him in instalments over the side of Jason's ship, causing the pious Colchians to stop and gather the bits for a decent interment. Medea once took sanctuary in Athens, having fled there in the chariot of the sun god, which she had drawn by dragons. Given women like this, or her aunt,

Circe, who was in the habit of turning shipwrecked sailors into pigs, it can be seen that witches are to be handled with care.

Even the great gods are not intrinsically benevolent (although they may become temporarily favourable with careful handling), and many minor spirits are actively malevolent. Their attentions may be warded off with charms, which is why many of the citizens of the most rational city on the planet sport Egyptian or Hebrew amulets. These bear exotic inscriptions, or contain magical objects such as the (alleged) bones of a shipwrecked man, or the blood of a condemned murderer.

Superstition remains a powerful force. Perikles once had to overcome the objections of a superstitious steersman who considered it bad luck to sail during an eclipse. Perikles did this by putting his cloak in front of the man's face, and patiently explaining that 'it's like this, but bigger, and further away'.

It is not only the ignorant peasants who feel this way. One might come across a grinning group of Athenians who have paused to watch Nikias, politician and military commander, hastily appease the gods, for example by spitting into his lap if he beheld an epileptic. (Indeed, Nikias' superstitious hesitation after an eclipse of the moon will later bring the Athenians to military disaster in Sicily.) Superstition drove the irritated Theophrastos to write: 'If a mouse gnaws into a bag of his grain, [a superstitious man] will ask the official diviner of omens what to do about it. If he is told "take the bag to a cobbler and get it sewn up," he will ignore this and seek to free himself from the portent by sacrificing at all the temples. He'll be constantly purifying his house, alleging that terrible Hekate has been spirited within. And if an owl hoots while he is outside, he gets terribly agitated, and won't go a step further before chanting loudly, "Oh Mighty Athena!" You will never see him step on a tomb, go near a dead body or a woman in childbirth: he tells you that everywhere there is a risk of pollution.'

While such men exist, there will always be business for those dealers in potions, amulets, herbs and charms. Many do not do their business in the Agora, but can be found after discreet enquiry, often doing brisk trade from dark alleyways in the Piraeus.

I dedicate to those [spirits] of the underworld Aristaichmos the smith and Pyrrhias, and his work and their souls. Also Sosias of Lamia, and his work and soul, and everything that they say and do. And the same goes for Hagesis of Boeotia.

This curse was written on a lead tablet and put into the wall of a house in the Street of the Marbleworkers near the Agora. (Hagesis evidently managed to offend the curser just in time to make it on to the curse as a postscript.) Similar curses are available at reasonable rates, if you know where to ask. Remember also that witchcraft generally is not illegal, but formally cursing people is.

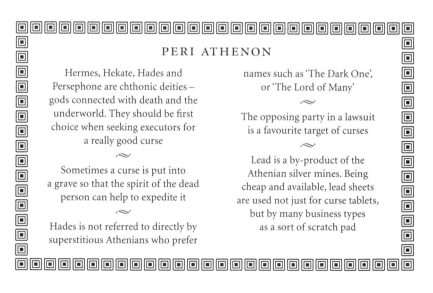

PERI ATHENON

Hermes, Hekate, Hades and Persephone are chthonic deities – gods connected with death and the underworld. They should be first choice when seeking executors for a really good curse

~

Sometimes a curse is put into a grave so that the spirit of the dead person can help to expedite it

~

Hades is not referred to directly by superstitious Athenians who prefer names such as 'The Dark One', or 'The Lord of Many'

~

The opposing party in a lawsuit is a favourite target of curses

~

Lead is a by-product of the Athenian silver mines. Being cheap and available, lead sheets are used not just for curse tablets, but by many business types as a sort of scratch pad

VIII · RITES OF PASSAGE

Military Service § *Funerals*
Weddings

MILITARY SERVICE

ASK AN ATHENIAN IF THE CITY is at peace, and the answer will be 'with whom?' In Greece at this time, one makes peace with a particular enemy just to make time to go fighting somewhere else. If there are no enemies available locally, then this is the perfect excuse to go looking for trouble further afield. In short, war is a way of life. Anyone staying with an Athenian male will probably have been invited to make appreciative noises at the host's panoply. This gleaming armour, prominently displayed, consists of a breastplate, a helmet covering most of the face, and greaves which protect the calves and shins. Then there is the large, circular shield, the *hoplon*, which gives this citizen warrior his name. As a hoplite an Athenian male is part of an army over 30,000 strong, and because these same hoplites in civilian dress make up the Athenian assembly, the democracy cannot be overthrown unless the army is defeated.

All able-bodied Athenian males aged between 17 and 59 do military service. However, not all can afford a panoply, so those who can afford one display it proudly – a panoply marks membership of the top two classes of citizenry, the

hippeis (aristocrats) and the *zeugetai* (those who produce more than a certain amount of corn). Those who cannot afford this kit are *thetes*. Some *thetes* have just a spear and shield, and fight as lighter-armed troops called *peltasts*. However, in Athenian democracy there is a place for everyone who wants to fight, and those who can't afford such

Dressed to kill. A hoplite in full panoply.

Unlike those of the regimented Spartans, Athenian shields sport a variety of motifs.

themselves to the deme council for enrolment as *ephebes*. This enrolment is not just into the army but also into the ranks of participating Athenian citizenry, and consequently is a very serious business. Anyone enrolling under false credentials can be sold into slavery. At the gymnasium and while on garrison duty these young men are taught the rudiments of drill and the use of the spear and shield. (Hoplites pack a sword as well, although this is used only when the tightly ordered battleline has broken down in victory or defeat.)

At special ceremonies one might see an Athenian being awarded a panoply by the state. This may be for exceptional bravery in battle, or because his father

weapons go to war with just a cushion – which is placed on the rowing bench of a trireme. Athens owes its military reputation to its naval fleet, and rowers are not slaves but free men, who are proud of their role. Mocking rowers or their contribution can easily lead to the discovery that anyone who spends up to 12 hours a day at the oar packs quite a punch.

Veteran soldiers and those under the age of 19 do garrison duty in Athens and Attica, while the rest of the men are on active military service. In consequence it is a rare Athenian who is fat or unfit, since even in this relatively humane city most disabled babies are 'discarded' at birth, and military training keeps the remainder in good shape. Every year in the demes of Attica young men present

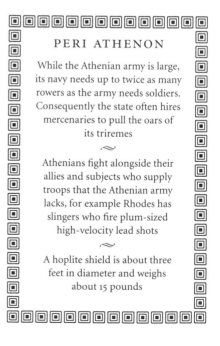

PERI ATHENON

While the Athenian army is large, its navy needs up to twice as many rowers as the army needs soldiers. Consequently the state often hires mercenaries to pull the oars of its triremes

~

Athenians fight alongside their allies and subjects who supply troops that the Athenian army lacks, for example Rhodes has slingers who fire plum-sized high-velocity lead shots

~

A hoplite shield is about three feet in diameter and weighs about 15 pounds

died fighting for Athens, and the city is replacing the fallen father's lost or damaged kit.

FUNERALS

AFTER A BATTLE, IT it is usual for the winners to erect a trophy – namely the arms of an enemy soldier mounted on a tree stump, showing that as victors, those who erected the trophy control the battlefield. In civilized places such as Greece, the victors will allow heralds of the enemy to come and arrange collection of their fallen, so that the bodies might be taken to their homes for burial.

They'll bury both of us in Kerameikos. We'll get it done and have the public pay. Tell the generals we died in battle, fighting in the ranks.

ARISTOPHANES
THE BIRDS • 510

Athenians gather every winter for the dolorous yet proud ceremony of interring the bones of those who have died in war. For two days the bones of the dead are kept in a tent, where family members and others who wish to do so place offerings by the remains. Then the bones are placed in large coffins of cypress wood, one for each tribe. A special coffin, empty yet richly decorated, commemorates those whose bodies could not be recovered. Anyone who wishes can join the dark-clad procession of the public funeral, which leads to the *demosion sema*, the military graveyard near the Kerameikos, an area described by Thucydides as 'the most beautiful place in Athens outside the walls'. There, just before the bones are interred, one of the foremost citizens of the city is invited to come forward and make a speech on behalf of the families of the fallen in praise of their dead. It is a solemn and moving occasion. Not for nothing do many vases show a woman helping her husband or son in the donning of his armour before battle. Everyone knows that this could be the first step to the final parting that occurs at this ceremony.

A military funeral has much in common with other funerals, which can be seen on a daily basis in Athens and Attica. A funeral is a ritual of Athenian life, a drama in three parts. The

Woman's gravestone, showing the deceased with a maidservant.

Grieving relatives pay their respects to the dead.

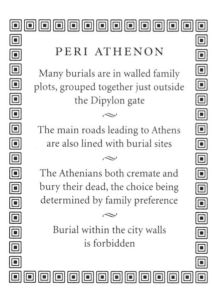

PERI ATHENON

Many burials are in walled family plots, grouped together just outside the Dipylon gate

~

The main roads leading to Athens are also lined with burial sites

~

The Athenians both cremate and bury their dead, the choice being determined by family preference

~

Burial within the city walls is forbidden

first act is private, during which the body is laid out and ritually purified by the women of the family. The body is washed and anointed, and the eyes closed to allow the release of the psyche from the body.

The deceased is crowned in flowers and wears an ankle-length garment to receive those who have come to pay final respects.

> *On two days a wife makes her man happy – the day he marries her, and the day he buries her.*
>
> CONTEMPORARY PROVERB ATTRIBUTED TO HIPPONAX OF EPHESUS

The second part of the funeral, the *ekphora*, happens before dawn on the third day, when the deceased is taken to the final resting place, usually in a cart. The burial is open to any who wish to attend, and is accompanied by songs and funeral dances. After this the women hurry away to prepare for the final act, the *perideipnon*, or funeral party.

WEDDINGS

For someone so in love with his new bride you're spending far too long outside her home.

Vase showing a wedding procession.

Go act married. The gods will see to it your marriage will change into one of those which makes you wish you'd turned it down.

MEDEA IN EURIPIDES • *MEDEA* • 743

IF FUNERALS TAKE PLACE BEFORE the dawn, weddings – which seem almost deliberately to turn funeral ritual into its mirror image with a happy celebration of life – occur in the evenings. Every visitor to Athens will at some point come across a wedding, since like almost every public event in Athens, this involves a procession or two. In this case the first is a noisy, good-humoured affair, in which the participants are generally tipsy from the wedding banquet. This includes a traditional large flat cake of pounded sesame seeds roasted and mixed with honeycake, all washed down copious amounts of wine. After an afternoon's partying, the bride is escorted from the house of her father to that of her husband. She stands in a richly decorated chariot, with her mother beside her, who lights the way with a torch. Behind come the families of the happy couple, and musicians making as loud a din as possible to scare away unfriendly spirits (melody is generally considered optional).

In her new home, the bride eats a quince or an apple, demonstrating that her husband's table is now her own. The happy couple are showered with fruit and nuts, which are both symbols of fertility and the ingredients for a healthy post-nuptial breakfast. The fruit shower

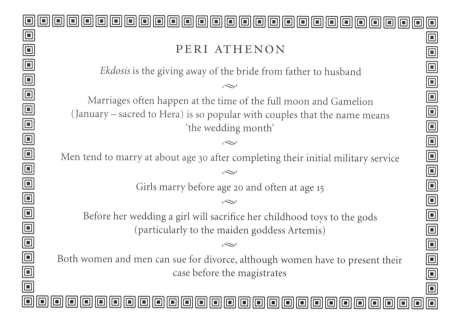

PERI ATHENON

Ekdosis is the giving away of the bride from father to husband

~

Marriages often happen at the time of the full moon and Gamelion
(January – sacred to Hera) is so popular with couples that the name means
'the wedding month'

~

Men tend to marry at about age 30 after completing their initial military service

~

Girls marry before age 20 and often at age 15

~

Before her wedding a girl will sacrifice her childhood toys to the gods
(particularly to the maiden goddess Artemis)

~

Both women and men can sue for divorce, although women have to present their
case before the magistrates

is a general hint about the process of reproduction, and bride and groom thereafter retire to try their hand at the business for themselves while their friends sing bawdy songs outside the door (a custom known as the *Epithalamium*). The next morning, the bride is a *gamos*, a woman confirmed in her nuptial status. This is the signal for another procession to make its way to the newlyweds' house. Those in the procession carry gifts to get the pair started on their married life. Baskets of fruit, combs, mirrors and practical items such as furniture are all donated. All the gifts have been chosen carefully, as they must reflect the status of the givers and their relationship with the newlywed couple.

IX · MUST-SEE SIGHTS

*In the Agora: the Bouleuterion • the Tholos •
the Royal Stoa • the Stoa of Zeus Eleuthereos •
the Hipparcheion • the Painted Stoa •
the South Stoa § On the Acropolis: the Propylaea •
the Erechtheion • the Parthenon*

*The beautiful and far-famed
city of Athens ...*

PLUTARCH • *LIFE OF THESEUS* • 1

IN THE AGORA

A NY VISITOR TO ATHENS IS obliged to visit the Agora. Many of the roads lead to it, or at least pass through it, and it is the social meeting place, noticeboard and shopping centre of the city. It is worth taking the time to see the Agora as a whole and having a slow stroll through the sights, studying the buildings and the history which the Athenians seem to take so much for granted.

*Holy Athens ...
and the famous, richly
adorned Agora*

PINDAR
*DITHYRAMB FOR THE
ATHENIANS* • FRAG 75

At first glimpse the Agora is a chaotic place. There is constant bustle as the Athenians go about their business, or meet to discuss politics, philosophy or the latest scandal. There are shrines set almost at random amid the large, open colonnades that protect the visitor from winter winds and summer sun. From here one can admire the towering Acropolis, or watch parades, athletic events and theatrical performances staged in the Agora's open space. But to understand the Agora and its central role in Athenian life, it is essential to know what is where and the different functions of each area.

Choose a quiet evening in late summer for your walk through the city, when the crowds have largely dispersed and the air is fragrant with the scent of woodsmoke and cooking. Position yourself at the porch of the Hephaisteion on a small hill west of the Agora. Mount Lykabettos peeps over the walls to the left, and from behind you the shadow of the great temple of Hephaestos points towards the Acropolis, where the Parthenon gleams with silver and gold in the setting sun. This walk will go from the Agora's administrative area, through the commercial area towards the Acropolis, the city's spiritual home.

Just down the slope from the Hephaisteion are four rows of dark, saffron-yellow stone, set into the hillside like an array of oversized steps. There is seating here for about 200 people. This

Northwest corner of the Agora, showing the Royal Stoa and one corner of the Painted Stoa.

mini-auditorium stands beside some of the main council offices of the city and is a useful forum for functionaries to present reports to the relevant committees.

A few yards from here lies a small ruined temple which was burned by the Persians and never restored. This was dedicated to Rhea, the mother of all the gods, including Zeus himself. Worship of the Great Mother was transferred to a building nearby, the **Bouleuterion**, in which stands her statue – another that is owed to the genius of Phidias (p. 64).

The Bouleuterion is famous not only for the statue (which shows the seated goddess with a cymbal in her hand and lions beneath her throne), but also because this is the record office of Athens. Rhea is the protector of records, and in her keeping are all the laws of Athens, records of lawsuits, financial accounts, lists of citizens and the official set of weights and measures used to keep the market traders honest.

The Bouleuterion not only serves as a home for Rhea and all that she protects.

View across the Agora looking towards the Acropolis.

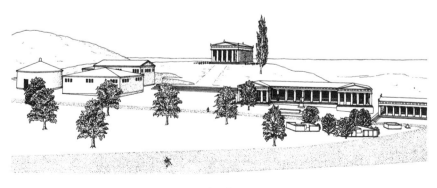

PERI ATHENON

In later years the Bouleuterion will become known as the Metroon, or old Bouleuterion, with the new building located uphill just behind it

~

The word *boule* comes from the Greek word meaning 'to decide after deliberation'

~

Within ten days of birth, all children of Athenian citizens must be registered in the Bouleuterion

~

The word 'agora' comes from the verb *ageiro*, meaning 'gather' or 'assemble'

~

The masonry storm drain of the Agora flows into the Eridanos. It will still be working perfectly in 2,500 years time

~

If a building is described as being of Pentelic marble, this means that the marble is of high quality and quarried from Mount Pentelikon, in Attica

the **Tholos**, although Athenians generally refer to it as the 'sun hat' (*skias*) because it has the same round shape. Here you might see assembly officials sitting down to a meal – typically of cheese, barley cakes, olives, leeks and wine, although if the city is going through prosperous times the officials might have meat or fish as well. The simple black-glazed crockery is marked with a clear DE (for *demosion*, or public property), to ensure that none of the diners accidentally bring a cup or two home from work.

The road running from left to right at this point is the main road leading to the Piraeus gate. Following this road will take you southwest past the Strategeion, where the military leaders of Athens sit

One of the stones which mark the boundary to the Agora.

It is the meeting place of the *boule*, the committee that decides the agenda for meetings of the assembly of the Athenian people. The *boule* has 500 members in all. Fifty are on duty at any one time, and indeed 17 actually sleep nearby, so that the city always has a body of men at its heart, ready to take control in any emergency. Beside the Bouleuterion, on the right, is a building officially called

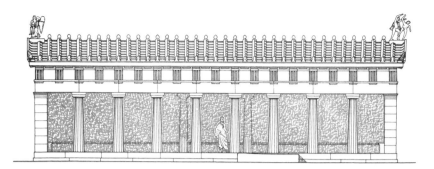

Front view of the Royal Stoa.

in council, and eventually past the prison. The Athenians are not much in favour of long incarcerations, preferring fines, exile, or if they feel the crime merits it, death. Therefore the prison is not a large building, and is in part an apothecary, where fatal doses of hemlock are measured out for administration to the miscreants held in the rooms next door. The prison is outside the formal boundary of the Agora. The Agora stops at the little cobbler's shop in the corner, beside which stands one of the marble shafts which marks the border. Each of these shafts carries an inscription saying 'I am the boundary of the Agora' in order to put the matter beyond question (p. 111).

Turn now in the opposite direction and walk back past the Bouleuterion to the **Royal Stoa** of the king of Athens. Yes, democratic Athens has a king, and although the *basileus* is nominally the second-in-command of the Athenian

> *They set the laws up at the Royal Stoa ... the nine archons [high city officials] took their oaths on the stone.*
>
> ARISTOTLE
> POLITICS • 7.1–2

government, his functions are mainly religious, with some legislative duties thrown in. Nor is the title hereditary (the holder is elected annually), so Athens has no princes or queens. Anyone wanting to check the legal position on any issue tends to come to the Royal Stoa, because the laws are carved into stone and positioned here – either as freestanding slabs or on the walls. In front is the 'Royal Stone', an ancient and un-adorned block of masonry on which incoming city officials swear their oaths before taking office.

The Royal Stoa looks slightly tatty beside the gleaming Pentelic marble of the newly built **Stoa of Zeus Eleuthereos** which stands next to it. Even now workmen are putting the finishing touches to the building, and painters are working on the magnificent frescoes, which include battle scenes, and (inevitably) yet more of the deeds of all-pervading

Theseus. Zeus Eleuthereos is the Zeus of freedom, the god who gave the Athenians liberty from the Persians and victory in the wars that followed. Although this is an administrative building – a stoa, not a temple – the Athenians felt that Zeus deserved something special in his name, and this was chosen. Stoas are often used for legal cases (though not for homicide cases which must be heard in the open). One comic writer remarks you can buy anything in this corner of the Agora, including figs, roses, water-clocks – and witnesses. Witnesses are much in demand, because the people of the city are quick to go to law if provoked, and it does not take much to provoke an Athenian. Top advocates get a much larger audience than just the jury, as the populace are connoisseurs of rhetoric and turn out in large numbers to hear their favourites perform.

Cicadas chirp up in the trees a month or two, but our Athenians keep chirping over lawsuits all their lives.

ARISTOPHANES
THE BIRDS • 40

Walk along this road further to the crossroads and the accompanying shrine. Near here is the **Hipparcheion**, headquarters of the aristocratic Athenian cavalry. In fact those coming down the Panathenaic Way on practice days need to keep a sharp eye out for oncoming horsemen, as they use the road for their drills. Most people do not mind, because the Hipparcheion

also provides free slapstick comedy in the form of neophytes learning to mount and dismount in a hurry. In a world innocent of stirrups, there are not a few tumbles and spills, even though the Athenian cavalry horse is considerably smaller than later breeds. For more formal displays, special stands called *ikria* are erected for spectators. These displays are well worth watching, especially if they include a race in which the contestants have to leap on and off a fast moving chariot whilst wearing full armour.

Avoid drinking from the well near the Hipparcheion. The water has a high lead content, as used records – printed on thin lead strips – are often dumped in here. If you need refreshment, go instead to the beautiful Enneakrounos fountain house, and drink your fill of fresh spring-water from the lion-headed spouts.

We were delayed by the crowd at the fountain-house, and in the jostle and crush the boldly tattooed slaves knocked pitchers right and left as they barged to the front of the queue.

ARISTOPHANES
LYSISTRATA • 330

There is a definite equine atmosphere to the Hipparcheion part of the Agora, and not just because the deposits left by excited horses may not have been completely swept away. The decorations on nearby buildings have bas reliefs of cavalry on parade or in action. One shows a squad in formation, with the leader in front and the second-in-command at

[113]

the rear, so the team can change leaders and direction to meet a new threat by simply turning their horses 180 degrees, yet still stay in their ranks.

In this location you will also find one of the most famous buildings in contemporary Athens. The **Painted Stoa** occupies perhaps the most favoured spot on the Agora, looking down the broad sweep of the Panathenaic Way, facing the gentle warmth of the winter sun even as its solid rear wall blocks the cold northerly wind. The stoa is an eclectic mixture of materials and styles, being built from marble and different types of limestone, with severe Doric columns outside and the more decorative Ionian pillars within. Officially this edifice is called the Peisianaktios, after the man responsible for building it. Regrettably for his reputation with posterity, Peisianax did all too good a job when he commissioned the magnificent paintings on the wooden panels that adorn this building. Now everyone simply calls it the Painted Stoa, and well does it deserve the name.

The top artists in Athens were engaged for these paintings. There is plenty of red paint, as the general theme is Athens victorious in battle over enemies both recent and mythological. Fights with Amazons and Trojans are shown, but pride of place goes to a mural of the battle of Marathon, depicting the moment when the Persian battleline was beginning to break.

There are also more tangible relics of Athenian martial valour displayed here,

for the Athenians like to hang a representative selection of shields taken from their defeated foes on the battlefield. (Spartan shields, with their distinctive inverted V, are given particular prominence.) There is always a crowd in this stoa. Among those to avoid bumping into are beggars, jugglers, pickpockets, sausage-sellers and Socrates. The Painted Stoa is a favoured hang-out of philosophers, and here Zeno of Kiteon will later teach stoicism, the philosophy named after this building.

Go a bit further down the Panathenaic Way, the wide street which runs diagonally across the Agora, and pause to admire the Altar of the Twelve Gods. This is the point from which distances from Athens are measured, and from where those fleeing for their lives make their appeal for sanctuary. This ancient altar is a reminder that this area was in use long before it became the market and administrative centre of Athens. Ancient peoples who are hardly remembered even in legend sank wells here, and used the Agora as a burial ground. The superstitious Athenians, who fear to tread on a grave, walk unknowing every day over the skeletons of their ancestors.

Now cross the open space in the middle of the Agora. On market days this is generally filled with temporary stalls, and on other days often features a variety of al fresco entertainments. This area marks the rough divide between buildings on the west and north which are primarily administrative, and those in the south and east, which are mainly

Finding sanctuary at the Altar of the Twelve Gods.

commercial. However, the market officials have their offices in the South Stoa, and, as we have seen, the other stoas on the north side are hardly innocent of commercial activity. Therefore the switch between administration and business across the Agora is not clear-cut, but a change of the flavours in the melange.

The **South Stoa** is another product of the Athenian building boom, so new that the paint has barely dried. The long double colonnade of this shopping mall is so elegant that one hardly notices a certain economy in the sun-dried mud-brick of the upper walls, and a restrained use of the marble used so lavishly in the state buildings on the other side of the Agora. There are a number of small rooms lining the back of the colonnade. The doors of these are slightly off-centre, the better to fit a dining couch on one side, since some of the traders here are not going to miss the chance of a good bit of business by going home for lunch, and indeed may plan to close a deal over lunch itself.

Beside the South Stoa stands a small building where the official weights were probably cast. This is the state foundry, which produces items such as oil lamps and the few bronze coins that the silver-rich currency requires. In later years this building will become the official mint.

Finally, for those who can't get enough of Theseus – and it seems that most Athenians cannot – it is worth over-shooting the Agora by a few hundred

PERI ATHENON

The water of the Enneakrounos is so pure that it is used for the ritual bathing of Athenian brides on their wedding day

~

The aristocratic cavalrymen of Athens often wear their hair longer than the average citizen

~

In a century's time Diogenes the Cynic, an advocate of extreme poverty, will often use the Stoa of Zeus for overnight accommodation

~

The inverted V on a Spartan shield is the Greek letter *lambda*, for 'Lakedaimon', the area around Sparta

yards to the east, and looking for the Theseion, the combined tomb and sanctuary of the all-Athenian hero. Legend says that Theseus died on the island of Skyros, and it was only recently that the Athenians made a major effort to find his bones. They eventually came across a large skeleton buried in the ancient style on the island, and brought the bones back to Athens. His tomb is now decorated with scenes from Theseus' major battles, painted by the best artists of the day. Because Theseus protected the poor and dispossessed, slaves in trouble with their masters and those oppressed by the powerful often take shelter here.

Athens is fairly strict with its architects, which is no bad thing given that so many are working here at present. A five-man committee overseen by the assembly supervises the process, and architects are supposed to work more for the prestige than the money. Anyone given a grant for work on a building has his fee sequestered, and has to account for where every drachma went (a list of these

KNOW YOUR MEASURES

A **stater** • (about 28 ounces) – indicated by a knucklebone

A ¼ **stater** • (just over 6.8 ounces) – indicated by a shield

A ⅙ **stater** • (4.5 ounces)– indicated by a turtle

(These should be stamped on to the weights, and if they are not, ask for official measures, on which they certainly are.)

A set of official weights as shown by the demos *printed on the side.*

costs is made public afterwards). If costs overrun by more than 25%, the excess comes out of the builder's commission.

The Agora will become more crowded in later years as new leaders of politics and commerce adorn the space with monuments to their memory. But the Agora of 431 BC can boast ornaments that will never be seen again. Perikles, Socrates, Thucydides and Sophocles walk its streets and patronize its wine-shops. If Athens is the city leading the world into tomorrow, the Agora is the beating heart which powers that city.

ON THE ACROPOLIS

IT IS A COMMON MISCONCEPTION among visitors that the Acropolis is the Parthenon. This is not so – the Parthenon is a temple on the Acropolis, while 'Acropolis' refers to the hill, and to the combined religious complex, fortress and state treasury on that hill. Many Greek cities have an Acropolis, but there is only one Parthenon.

To start a tour of the Acropolis, go around the hill to the western slope. One of the very best times for this is just as winter turns to spring, when the air is crisp, and every ridge and outcrop of the hill is bursting with wild flowers. Look for the wide, sweeping staircase that leads up the Acropolis to the **Propylaea**. This is literally the 'fore-gate' (*pro* means 'before' and *pylae* means 'gates'). Although it seems as though the basic purpose of this structure is to suitably impress visitors before

they even get to see the other wonders of the hill, the Propylaea is a real gateway. As Pausanias explains:

This is the only entrance to the Acropolis. There is no other because the hillside is so steep and has a fortified wall besides.

PAUSANIAS • *DESCRIPTION OF GREECE* 1.22.4

The Propylaea is a substantial building in its own right, and in fact has a small art gallery in a room on the left of the actual gateway. The ceiling is of white Pentelic marble, with grey Eleusinian marble added in places for extra effect. Because the entire Acropolis is both a functional fortress and a work of art, the Doric theme of the Parthenon is echoed in the Propylaea, and the columns of this gateway have the same proportions as those of the temple. In fact even the steps on which the columns rest are carefully proportionate to the rest of the gateway, with aesthetically pleasing areas picked out in white marble, and the remainder blended into the background with grey. Mnesikles, a colleague of Phidias, is the architectural genius largely responsible for this design.

Escaped slaves, miscreants, the unpurified and general riff-raff get no further than this. There are at least two good reasons for checks at this point. First, the Athenian treasury is within, and secondly, anyone with crimes on his conscience can head straight for the appropriate shrine, claim sanctuary and escape justice. (Once you claim

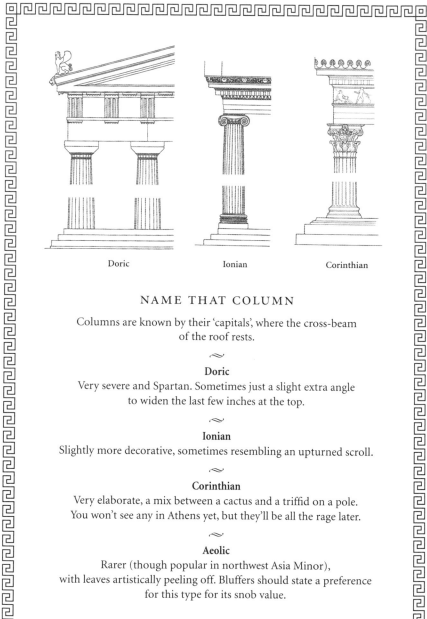

Doric   Ionian   Corinthian

NAME THAT COLUMN

Columns are known by their 'capitals', where the cross-beam
of the roof rests.

~

Doric
Very severe and Spartan. Sometimes just a slight extra angle
to widen the last few inches at the top.

~

Ionian
Slightly more decorative, sometimes resembling an upturned scroll.

~

Corinthian
Very elaborate, a mix between a cactus and a triffid on a pole.
You won't see any in Athens yet, but they'll be all the rage later.

~

Aeolic
Rarer (though popular in northwest Asia Minor),
with leaves artistically peeling off. Bluffers should state a preference
for this type for its snob value.

sanctuary at a shrine, you are under the protection of the god.)

After a quick mental check that you do not have any unpurged murders, escapes from slavery or general mayhem on your conscience, enter the gate and turn right. Head for the small shrine to Athena Nike, the exquisite little building raised in thanks for victory over the Persians. Remember to bring some honey-cakes or flowers to lay at the altar so that the goddess will forgive the main reason for this visit – to savour the stunning view across Athens, past the Piraeus to where the triremes and merchant ships crowd the entrance to the harbours. On a clear day – and the Attic air often has an enchanting, magical clarity – the islands of the Saronic gulf lie sun-burned brown in a turquoise sea, and the pale grey mountains of the Peloponnese line the distant horizon.

The temple itself is a small gem, with Ionic columns and friezes all around the walls. The bas reliefs have the usual theme of Athenians victorious in battle, although the stone depictions of slaughter seem forced and unnatural against the serene panorama all around. When sated with the view (expect this to take some time) move northwards once more, towards the temple of Athena Polias, sometimes called the **Erechtheion** – possibly after a legendary king of that name. As an inscription shows, at one time there were 110 people of different ages, skill and social class, all working on the Erechtheion for the flat rate of a drachma a day. This temple has

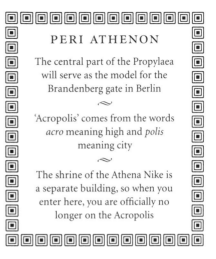

PERI ATHENON

The central part of the Propylaea will serve as the model for the Brandenberg gate in Berlin

~

'Acropolis' comes from the words *acro* meaning high and *polis* meaning city

~

The shrine of the Athena Nike is a separate building, so when you enter here, you are officially no longer on the Acropolis

been mentioned in connection with the Panathenaia (p. 87). It was here that Athena and Poseidon competed to become patron of Athens. Poseidon smote the rock (one can see the mark of the trident by which Poseidon is identified) and a spring burst forth. Athena in reply gave an olive tree, the first of its kind, which grows in the small garden outside near the wall. They say that when the Persians destroyed the Acropolis they burned this tree, but within a day it was sprouting again.

Once more, expect to spend some time here. The entire building is in the Ionic style, in elegant contrast to the severe form of the nearby Doric Parthenon. Its effortless lines initially hide the fact that the builders had to complete a set of architectural gymnastics to construct the building while still respecting the pre-existing sacred places of various gods in this part of the hill. So not only

Athena, but also Zeus, Poseidon, Hermes and Hephaestos are represented in this small temple – yet space has still been found to cram in further sundry demi-gods and heroes. If the atmosphere becomes unbearably sacred, bolt for the outer porch. Plato will later claim that there is a perfect form of everything, of which all other versions are inferior copies. This is the perfect porch. As with almost everything on the Acropolis, designers and mathematicians were at work before the first chisel was lifted, and the result of all the thought and effort seems utterly natural and effortless, with everything so obviously right that it is impossible to imagine it done differently. One gets to share the view with six beautiful maidens. These are made of stone, and serve as pillars

(*caryatids*). They support the roof on their heads, although their relaxed poses make it plain that this is no effort, and they are quite happy to keep doing it for the next few thousand years. Mountains – northerly Parnes, nearby Lykabettos and distant Hymettos – line the horizon, while the green and golden-brown expanse of Attica sweeps up to the city walls. Below to the left, tiny figures scuttle, ant-like, about the Agora, and the noise of the city sounds faint and remote. You might never want to leave.

The best, however, has been saved for last. It is time to approach the crown jewel of the Acropolis, the **Parthenon**, temple of the maiden goddess Athena, by common consent the most beautiful building in the world. Of course, the Parthenon starts with a natural

A first view of Athena Promachos and the Parthenon from the Propylaea.

The most beautiful building in the world, the Parthenon of the Acropolis.

advantage. Given the jaw-dropping beauty of the surrounding view and the co-ordinated architectural splendour in which it is set, it would be worth climbing the Acropolis hill to visit even if the Parthenon were a dung-heap, and not, as it truly is, a temple which gloriously surpasses the wonders around it.

This will not be the visitor's first sight of the Parthenon. To anyone in Athens it is always there, a serene jewel atop the hillside, with the occasional flash as the sun glances off the shield or spear of the gigantic statue of Athena Promachos nearby. But suddenly, when one is right beside the Parthenon, the building seems huge. Seventeen massive marble columns stretch along the side, irresistibly drawing the view heavenward to the shadowed friezes just below the roof. The Parthenon is impressive, monumentally and comprehensively so, although it takes an architect's eye to

pick out how deliberately and systematically this effect has been achieved.

The columns are indeed towering, but they taper slightly towards the top, fooling the eye into giving them the height of much taller columns seen from the same perspective. The corner columns are about two inches wider than the others, and set somewhat closer to those beside them, giving the impression of foreshortening through greater distance. And the entire structure is not quite upright, but leans imperceptibly inward, as a sheer cliff face appears to do as one leans back to take it all in. The front is eight columns wide, whereas the standard for this type of temple is six, so once again a viewer forms the impression that the Parthenon is bigger than the space it occupies. Yet because it appears larger than it is, the Parthenon achieves a soaring elegance, as the bulky reinforcements the mind unconsciously

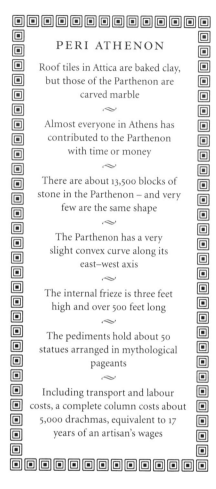

PERI ATHENON

Roof tiles in Attica are baked clay, but those of the Parthenon are carved marble

~

Almost everyone in Athens has contributed to the Parthenon with time or money

~

There are about 13,500 blocks of stone in the Parthenon – and very few are the same shape

~

The Parthenon has a very slight convex curve along its east–west axis

~

The internal frieze is three feet high and over 500 feet long

~

The pediments hold about 50 statues arranged in mythological pageants

~

Including transport and labour costs, a complete column costs about 5,000 drachmas, equivalent to 17 years of an artisan's wages

have flesh tones, and embroidery and borders are painted on their robes. Even the walls are deep blue or brick red, an effect that works particularly well against the polished bronze of the temple doors. (When within the building remember to look up, and admire the exquisite decoration of the coffered ceiling, with every line and curve picked out in subtle colours.)

The overall effect on the exterior is of graceful, flowing lines of colourful, massive, yet somehow insubstantial masonry, pulling the visitor's attention to the colourful friezes which decorate the temple. At the eastern end we see Athena being born. Zeus sits enthroned in his majesty regarding the offspring sprung from his forehead, while Hephaestos stands beside her holding his axe, and the other Olympian gods observe with wonder this new addition to their pantheon. On the opposite, western side, we see again in pictorial form the contest by which Athena's olive won the patronage of the city against the trident of Poseidon.

Many visitors, intending to enter the temple, find themselves instead beguiled into walking around it, crab-style, as they study the sculptures; dynamic, perfectly imagined forms of a quantity and quality hardly existing anywhere in the known world. Centaurs and Amazons are engaged in battle, Greek warriors struggle with Persian bowmen, gods with giants. In the process one absorbs the Athenian message: that intellect triumphs over irrationality, civilization

expects are lighter and more delicate than seems possible.

Another effect of the Parthenon, particularly startling when seen up close, is that the building is not the austere white marble seen by later ages. It is a riot of colour. The external columns are painted light grey, and the interior columns are pale ochre. All the statues

Horsemen in Classical mode. The friezes depict an idealized reality, in which riding horses bareback whilst naked is safe and commonplace.

over barbarism, liberalism over totalitarianism. But, ironically, this message will be clouded in later ages when many of these friezes are vandalized beyond salvage by religious fanatics, and the Parthenon itself is almost wrecked by an explosion while being used as an ammunition depot. The victory over barbarism will remain uncertain, even millennia hence.

Yet the dynamism and optimism of the Athenians can be seen in the inner frieze, which shows the people of the city in procession to the temple, bearing gifts and sacrifices to the goddess. The celebrants are proud and joyful, and their manner is confident rather than humble, dignified rather than penitent. This frieze shows the city and its people as they see themselves, Athenians and their

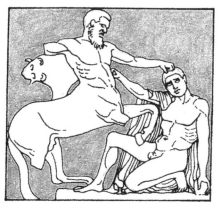

Metopes (above and right) showing centaurs battling the men of the Lapiths.

Centaurs are wise, kindly creatures, but turn murderous when drunk.

goddess meeting to mutually congratulate each other on a job well done.

Within the temple stands the representation of Athena Parthenos herself. The masterpiece of Phidias stands resplendent in gold and ivory. Even the statue of Victory which Athena holds in her right hand is larger than a man, while her spear seems to stretch to the heavens. Serene and majestic in her armour and helmet, the massive golden Athena is a stunning, awesome embodiment of the values that Athens represents and holds most dear.

Yet, for all its glory, the Parthenon is not the religious centre of the Acropolis – this role is taken by the Erechtheion. In the Parthenon Athena guards not just Athenian values but Athenian valuables – as previously mentioned her golden garments contain much of the state's gold reserves, and stashed away in this building are golden bowls, wreaths and dedications wrought in silver and encrusted with precious jewels. In times of need these can be sold or melted down to pay for the armies and triremes with which Athens sustains her empire. But now, with Athens largely at peace, revenues flow into the city in unprecedented amounts. Much of this bounty is being spent in building Athens into the leading city of Greece, but some of the money is being turned into treasure, and put aside for hard times to come. Athena, goddess of wisdom, must surely approve.

A representation of Helios, god of the sun, appears on the eastern pediment of the Parthenon. Helios' connection with Athena comes through his daughter Aurora, the goddess of the dawn. For when day breaks over Athens, the light of dawn first touches the eastern pediment, so that the Parthenon is shining gold and warm honey-brown whilst the city below is still deep in shadow.

And it is now – in the morning, filled with the optimism of a new beginning – which is probably the best time to leave the Parthenon and Athens itself, while the morning sunlight splashes over the Acropolis and Greece awakes to a new day.

USEFUL PHRASES

At the Symposium

I would love to come to the symposium with you, but I promised my mother I would help with her tapestry tonight.
egō soi pros to sumposion hekōn sunēkolouthoun an, ei mē hupeschomēn meta tēs mētros huphēnai tēsde tēs hesperās.

I'm sorry, we can either discuss the transcendent nature of states of being, or have more wine. I can't do both.
sungnōthi moi: ē gar peri tou ontos tou theiou exetazōmen ē pleion sumpînōmen. amphoterō gar hama poiein adunatō.

Indeed, I assure you that Homer's family name was Simpson.
ho dē Homēros ontōs ēn ho Simōnos.

Sophocles? Well, he's okay, but for a man who really knows his way around the iambic triameter, give me Aeschylus any day.
peri Sophokleous? ouk amathēs esti, all' ei tina entribestaton tois trimetrois iambois meterchēi, hairou pantapāsi ton Aischulon.

Quickly, bring me a beaker of wine, so that I may wet my mind and say something clever. (Aristophanes)
all', exenengke moi tacheōs oinou choā, ton noun hin' ardō kai legō ti dexion.

Listen carefully, speak seasonably.
akouson akribōs, eukairōs eipe.

So, Socrates, how's the missus?
ag' eipe moi, ō Sōkrates, pōs echei hē sou gunē?

About town

How much is that?
poson touto didōs?

It's too expensive!
tîmiōteron estin.

Give me back my money!
apodos moi to argurion.

I'm lost.
ouk oid' hopou gēs eimi.

Excuse me.
sungnōthi moi.

Can you help me please?
em', ei dokei, ōphēleseis?

This is something I picked up at the Agora.
toutî ēgorasa.

There was nowhere else to hang my hat, but I'll take it off the herm if it bothers you.
all' ouk edunamēn allothi to emou pîlidion tithenai, ei d' isōs touto chalepos phereis, auto ton Hermēn ekdūsō.

Is this the ferry to Salamis? If not, when can I stop rowing?
āra porthmeuometha pros tēn Salamîna? ei mē, pot' elaunein pauōmai?

That's three honeycakes, a bunch of violets and some fried fish to go please.
ekdot' emoi, ei dokei, treis melitoussās kai stephanon iōn kai phruktous ichthūs.

May Apollo make your olive groves, your sheep and your loins infertile!
parechoi ho Apollōn tās sās elaiās kai ta probata kai to sperma akarpa.

I'm looking for a second-hand Skythian, in good condition, for running errands and picking up the kids from school.
doulon tina zētō Skuthikon, entelē kateschēmenon ēd', hina pragmata te polla poiēi kai tous paidas ek tou didaskaleiou oikad' anagēi.

In the tavern
This is all Greek to me.
tauta pant' esti moi barbara.

Cheers!
propînō soi.

Give me a beer.
oinon ek krithōn pepoiēmenon ekchei moi.

How long must I wait?
poson chronon epimenō?

Look at the time!
pēnik' esti.

You are two hours late.
bradus ei miāi hōrāi.

Unhand my wife immediately, you drunken unpleasant fellow.
autik' aphes em', anthrōpe, hode gar ho emou anēr nîkēn en tōi Delphikōi palaismati enîkēsen.

Another round of olives please barman!
pleionas elaiōn echōmen, ō kapēle?

A Spartan, Athenian and Boeotian walk into a tavern...
Spartiatēs tis pote kai Athēnaios kai Boiōtos eis kapēleion badisantes ...

Is the wine meant to do this to the inside of the cup?
āra mē ho oinos tēn kulika houtōs blaptein philei?

Get your cloak honey, you've pulled.
analabe ton son chitōna, ō philtatē, eme gar erōti kēleis.

I've got to go. Someone call me a torch-bearer.
iteon d'esti moi: proskalei nun paida te kai lampada.

Discussing politics and philosophy
Never fight a land war in Asia Minor.
mēpote pros tēn Asiān polemēis.

Men's wishes are different from what god orders.
ta anthrōpōn boulēmata tōn theōn epitagmatōn diapherei.

What do you mean, I look Persian?
tini de tropōi son phainomai Persikos?

You have all the requirements for a politician: a horrible voice, bad breeding and a vulgar manner. (Aristophanes *Knights*, 217–18)
ta d'alla soi prosesti dēmagōgika, phōnēi miara, gegonas kako⁻s, agoraios ei.

Noble thoughts require noble language.
to kalōs theōrein axioi to kalōs legein.

General expressions
Where is the lyceum?
pou esti to Lukeion?

Where are you going?
poi badizeis?

Persians go home!
it' oikad', ō Persai.

Do you know how to do this?
oistha touto poiēsai?

Is that everything?
tout' exarkei?

Farewell!
chaire.

AUTHOR'S NOTE

Athens continued as an intellectual centre for many years after the start of the Peloponnesian war, but a time dating to just before the war began was chosen for this book, as it marks both the peak of Athenian splendour, and the point just before a certain innocence was lost.

As ever, there are many people who helped in bringing this work to publication. Special thanks are due particularly to John Camp, author of *The Athenian Agora* (1992) and *The Archaeology of Athens* (2004), the best modern surveys for the layperson and student, for giving unsparingly of his time and expertise; to David Butterfield for his help with the ancient Greek translations; and to Jackie Whalen, my student at the time, who helped with research materials. I would especially like to thank Ludwik and Krystyna Dziurdzik for their short but vital contribution, and I dedicate this book to them accordingly.

SOURCES OF ILLUSTRATIONS

a = above, b = below, l = left, r = right, t = top.

Agora Museum, Athens 47

akg-images/Peter Connolly 121; I–IV

akg-images/Erich Lessing 104

American School of Classical Studies at Athens 62t, 62b, 110t, 111, 112, 115, 116, 120

Antikensammlungen, Staatliche Museen zu Berlin 86, 103br

Archaeological Museum of Olympia 12

The Art Archive/Archaeological Museum, Istanbul, photo Dagli Orti 2

Ashmolean Museum, Oxford 41al, 55

Bibliothèque Nationale, Paris 16

British Museum, London 1, 6, 20, 30, 46, 48, 58, 69, 78, 79, 84, 85, 103, 109, 125; X

Peter Bull 20b

Cabinet des Médailles, Bibliothèque Nationale, Paris VIII, IX and XII

Mrs M. E. Cox from *The Parthenon and its Sculptures* by John Boardman,
       Thames & Hudson Ltd, 1985 123

École Française d'Athénes, reconstruction drawing after Fouilles de Delphes 10

after Gerhard, *Auserlesene Griechische Vasenbilder* 26

J. Paul Getty Museum, Malibu, California 76

after F. Krauss, 1943 118

Kunsthistorisches Museum, Vienna 54

Metropolitan Museum of Art, New York 21, 107

Musei e Gallerie Pontificie, Vatican XI

Museo Nazionale Archeologico, Taranto 75

Museo Nazionale, Ferrara VII

Museo Nazionale, Naples 60, 73; XIII

National Archaeological Museum, Athens 11, 74, 98, 105

Nationalmuseet, Copenhagen 41ar

Norbert Schimmel Collection, New York 17

Virginia Museum, Richmond XIV

All other line drawings are by Rhiannon Adam

INDEX